Training to Teach

TRAINING TO TEACH

A Basic Course in
Christian Education

HARRY G.
and BETTY L. GOODYKOONTZ

THE WESTMINSTER PRESS · *Philadelphia*

Library of Congress Catalog Card No. 61–10293

To
Our Three Children
Who Have Taught Us Much

Contents

Preface

In this little book we have endeavored to meet what we believe to be a great need—namely, to set forth, in language that laymen can understand, the current thinking concerning the nature of Christian education. This book grew out of a hand-tailored course in Bardstown Road Presbyterian Church, Louisville, Kentucky. For three years this material was taught each spring to the teachers and leaders who expected to begin their work in the fall, and to the teachers who were on rotation. It was also taught in a city leadership school under the auspices of the Louisville Area Council of Churches.

Our purpose has been to orient the members of the class to the current understanding of the importance, nature, goals, and fundamental principles of Christian education, and, against this background of the philosophy of Christian education, to help them see how the process and program of Christian education come alive in the particular church. This orientation course has been designed particularly for those who have not held leadership positions in Christian education, but it has been a good refresher course for experienced leaders.

The lectures and discussions were recorded on tape. This book reflects the direct and informal approach and language of the class. We have tried to be both clear and profound. The Presbyterian background of the authors is frankly acknowledged, but we believe this book can be used in churches of practically all denominations. This book can be read by an individual or used as a text in an orientation course on the foundations of Christian education. The material can be covered in a quarter, but with a little ingenuity on the part of the teacher the course can be expanded to two or three or four times that length. A year-round leadership education class could use this as a general guide, supplementing it with study of specific methods and elaborating upon certain topics at will.

We have written as a team. We have worked together for nearly thirty years. One of us is director of Christian education in a local church; the other is professor of Christian education in a Presbyterian theological seminary. We are particularly indebted to the teaching of Edward B. Paisley and W. Taliaferro Thompson, to practical experience under the wise guidance of John L. Fairly, and to the writings of Lewis J. Sherrill. Our indebtedness extends to a host of writers in all the theological disciplines. The bibliography suggests our indebtedness to writers in the field of Christian education but fails to reveal our great debt to Biblical and theological scholars as well as to educators and psychologists. Nor should we fail to express our thanks to the grand laymen who helped us so greatly by studying these foundations with us. The faithful and efficient work of Mrs. Katherine Wilson in preparing the manuscript made our task much easier. Portions of Chapters I to VI, in shorter form, first appeared as a series of articles in *The Earnest Worker,* July through December, 1953. Published by the Board of Christian Education, Presbyterian Church U.S., Richmond, Virginia. This material is used here by permission.

It is our prayer that many people will find this little book helpful.

B. L. G. AND H. G. G.

Louisville, Kentucky

I

The Nature of Christian Education

Christian education is an inescapable part of the work of the church. Any church that takes seriously the example and the teaching of Jesus will take Christian education seriously. Jesus left three things for his church to do: to preach, to teach, and to heal. These three are symbolized by the pulpit, the Sunday church school, and the pastoral ministry. In any church that is approximating the thought of the New Testament, you will find the gospel proclaimed from the pulpit and the sacraments administered; you will find people gathered in home or Sunday school or a small group to study the relationship of the Bible to themselves and to the world in which they live; and you will find the church ministering to the soul needs of its people as well as to their social needs. Christian education is important for one very simple reason: people need it if they are to grow in Christ.

There have been times in the history of the church—not its most brilliant periods—when people thought that all that was necessary was to get a man over the line, to lead him to say, "I take Jesus as my Savior." And then you could drop him. He was on his own. Maybe he would grow, maybe he would not. In many churches there existed this attitude that conversion was the one thing that was important. When you study the Bible carefully, it is obvious that he who is converted does not instantaneously become a perfect Christian. He who is converted still has to be nurtured in the Christian faith. He has to have its deeper meanings unfolded to him. He has to experience for himself what it means to grow in grace. Theologically, this is the doctrine of sanctification, which is nothing more nor less than growing and developing in one's Christian life by the work of the Holy Spirit. In this world

11

we do not reach perfection. We grow toward, but never reach, our goal, which is to be mature in Jesus Christ.

It is not enough, then, to lead a man across the line to salvation. To bring a man to Christ is just a beginning, not an end. To bring a man to Christ is to place him where he needs to be. But once he is there, he has to live there, and in that place he has to grow. It is the purpose and function of Christian education to enable man to grow into maturity in Christ.

Christian education is important, furthermore, because Jesus Christ said to his church, "Go . . . teach" (Matt. 28:16-20). To make a disciple is to teach. The church is under orders to help people to understand the gospel and to bring them into a vital relationship with Jesus Christ. Paul, writing to the church at Colossae, said: "Him [Christ] we proclaim, warning every man and teaching every man in all wisdom, that we may present every man mature in Christ. For this I toil, striving with all the energy which he mightily inspires within me" (Col. 1:28-29). This is probably the quotation which best sets forth the Biblical understanding of the nature of Christian education. This verse implies that our aim is to help every person in the church develop into a mature Christian. There is a seventeen-year-old maturity for a seventeen-year-old Christian, which is not the same as the maturity of a seventy-year-old, but there is a difference in the seventeen-year-old who is not mature in Christ and the seventeen-year-old who is mature in Christ. The goal, then, is to present every church member mature in Christ. This can be done only in the power of the Holy Spirit and not merely by human effort, but human effort is important. Christian education has endeavored to bring those people who are in the church into a deeper knowledge of the Lord. It has also endeavored to bring those who are outside the church into the church. It has had an evangelistic motive as well as a teaching motive. In the frontier days the Sunday school was primarily evangelistic in purpose. It is no longer primarily an evangelistic instrument, but it still has evangelism as a secondary function.

Any religion that lasts has to teach. One modern church leader said, "We teach or we die." Every living religion has been a teaching religion. No religion lasts that does not teach profoundly and continuously. The heritage must be passed on to the next generation.

The Christian religion, founded on one who was called the Master (or Teacher), certainly involves teaching. Deuteronomy, ch. 6, written hundreds of years before Christ, says that if the worship of the Lord God is to be meaningful, it must be taught in the home, and the Christian religion picks that up. When you have a serious belief in God, then you are bound to teach, and you start in your own home. The best Christian education ought to take place in the home. The main job of the church in its Christian education program is to teach adults, who in turn teach their own children and, to a lesser degree, the children of others. Teaching adults is the most important aspect of the teaching work of the church. Christian education is important because it is an inescapable part of the work of the church, because our Lord commanded it, because people need it, and because the church cannot live unless it teaches. One additional reason why Christian education is of enormous importance is that our kind of world is in desperate need of Christian teaching. This line of thought will be developed in the next chapter.

When asked what Christian education is, some people reply that it is teaching about Jesus; others say that it is teaching moral standards or teaching a way of life or teaching the Bible. From any standpoint, education is taking the heritage of the past and applying it to the present, with some implications for the future. We have to come to grips with our heritage and see what it means for us in our time. Any institution that would perpetuate itself must have a teaching program. This is true of the church as well as of the state. Any institution that would perpetuate itself must so understand its own fundamental ideals and purposes as to pass those purposes and ideals on to each succeeding generation. This the state does through the public schools. This the church must do through its own teaching program.

Christian education takes place within the setting of the Christian communities of home and church. Christian education is not limited to the Sunday church school and family training. In youth work, Christian nurture takes place. The young people's program is the effort of the church to deepen in its youth an understanding of the nature of the gospel as it relates to youth who live in the current age. Other phases of the program of Christian education are: church officer training; the men's fellowship; the women of the church, especially their circle groups; weekday religious education; and the heavy program of summer activities. For youth and adults the corporate worship service makes a major contribution to the Christian nurture of the faithful. Not least, as later chapters will show, Christian nurture occurs in the life of the nurturing communities.

Historically, there have been various concepts of the nature and purpose of Christian education. We cannot understand the present philosophy of Christian education unless we know something of what has been thought in the past. By the time the Sunday school movement reached America, around 1790, the main emphasis was on teaching the Bible and the catechism. It would be more accurate to say the emphasis was on memorization of Bible and catechism.

In the opening years of the nineteenth century, emphasis was primarily on memorization of the catechism. Insufficient attention was given to the meaning of what was memorized. Between 1810 and 1815, a shift was made to an emphasis on memorizing the Bible. That Sunday school was considered best in which the pupils memorized the most verses in a given period. Prizes were given to those who memorized the greatest number of Scripture verses. This *memoriter* period lasted fifteen years or so. Christian leaders failed to understand that a person could memorize half the Bible and still not be a Christian.

The first fifty years of Christian education in the formal sense in this country emphasized memory work. Then came a long period of half a century when nobody quite knew what the score was, when all kinds of curriculums were extant, and chaos reigned in the Sunday school. Each private publisher vied with each other private publisher to get as much income from the Sunday school market as was possible, without giving sufficient thought to the basic content of the curriculums. In 1872 the Uniform Lesson Series concept was adopted with enthusiasm and the curriculum chaos came to an end.

For more than seventy-five years the goal of the Sunday school was to teach the facts of the Bible. Linked with this was the kindred goal of evangelism. The Sunday school was largely an evangelistic agency. In some sections of the Ohio and Mississippi valleys the Sunday school preceded the ordained ministers, and Sunday schools preceded churches—with results not fully wholesome. For many years perhaps the main thought was that in Sunday school there was a lesson to be taught, and this lesson involved the Bible and a quarterly. To have a program of Christian education was to have a Sunday school where a lesson—at first ungraded —was to be taught.

At the turn of the century under the influence of John Dewey and his colleagues, the church schools began to recognize that emphasis is put in the wrong place when that which is taught is given priority over those who are taught. The person being taught is more important than what we teach him, so progressive educators insisted. "Content versus persons" became the main topic of discussion in educational circles. The implications of this discussion were not lost on Christian educators. They came to see clearly that it is not enough to teach the Bible; you must teach the Bible to persons. The main emphasis is on the persons, not on the material to be taught. This principle led inevitably to graded literature.

By the 1920's, the emphasis was placed on learning through experiences. Christian education was considered to be a matter of guided experiences in Christian living. Out of these guided experiences profound inner changes and growth in Christlikeness were expected to come.

In the last few years we have witnessed some fundamental changes in curriculum theory and in statements of the aims of Christian nurture. The truths inherent in the former emphases have been retained. Memorization suffered most, but today there is a renewed emphasis on the value of memorizing great Scripture passages, and as late as 1960 a Scottish theologian was pleading for a renewed but intelligent teaching of the great catechisms of the church. "Memorize with understanding." The Bible continues to be the main textbook of the Christian religion, and Biblical facts and stories continue to be taught. In "the age of the child" we are not likely to cease being "child-centered," in a sense. There can be no effective education without "experiences in Christian living." The evangelistic aim in modernized garb is still with us. But some significant changes have occurred.

We have gone back to a deeper understanding of theology, of the Bible, of church history, and we have analyzed more thoughtfully and more carefully the values and the weaknesses of the theories that are predominant in public education. There was a time when religious educators accepted as being good also in the

Sunday church school, every educational theory and practice that the psychologists and educators said was good in the public school. More recently, we have recognized that the two kinds of schools are not identical and that there are some philosophies and some aspects of training that are acceptable for Christian teaching purposes and some that are not acceptable. Not all methods are suitable to the teaching of the gospel.

In recent years tremendous changes have taken place in the understanding of the nature of Christian education. Whatever the professed aim of the publishers of religious materials, whatever the thinking of denominational boards of education, the average aim of the average teacher was either to teach the facts of the Bible or else to make people good. It is heresy to believe that we can "make people good." Of course we want pupils to become good, but when this is the primary purpose of teaching, it can easily become moralism. It is difficult to put the concept of moralism into words, but moralism is not hard to recognize in practice. Moralism forgets that one cannot lift one's self by one's own bootstraps. Moralism suggests that the man who lives the best life is the man who has the best chance of getting to heaven. Moralism ultimately is a denial of our need of a Savior, a denial of the Biblical faith. Moralism—"doing good" or "being good"—forgets that no one but God is good, and it forgets that such goodness as we have is a gift of God. The Christian does endeavor to live a life worthy of the gospel. But this is not to be identified with a lot of petty do's and don'ts.

Christian education is neither emphasis on content nor emphasis on persons; it is both—and more. It is through guided experience that we learn, but this experience has one basic purpose: to bring human beings into confrontation with God in Jesus Christ. The essence of the philosophy of Christian education is just this—a divine-human encounter—so that every teaching experience contributes to this goal, wherein teacher and pupil alike are aware of the presence of the living Lord, are aware of the divine-human encounter.

The process of Christian education endeavors to bring about a relationship between persons and God. The heart of the process of Christian nurture is the relationship between the persons and the living God. As part of the process of Christian education we should use the information that we have about life as it is today and life as God intends it to be, bringing this into the class situation. The Bible and all other teaching instruments—textbooks, quarterlies, audio-visuals, hymnbooks, prayer books, current literature, the morning newspapers, every source of inspiration and information that we can find—may be used in the process of education, that the relationship may be experienced more deeply and its meanings grasped more clearly. The teacher is likely to be the catalyzer in this educational process, but he too is caught up in the process, and he too may hope to meet God face to face from time to time in this teaching.

The fundamental purpose in teaching Sunday school is that the people in this class in this hour may have some vital experience with the living God. This is the purpose that differentiates the teaching of Christianity from the teaching of physics or chemistry. In teaching the Christian faith, the purpose is that boys and girls, men and women, may come closer to Christ, hear him speak through the words of Scripture, through the words of the members of the class as they share ideas, through the words and actions of the teacher. In the whole setting of the classroom the effort is to bring the class into a dynamic relationship with God.

Once in Christian education the Bible was considered to be central: "We teach the Bible." But a person can know the Bible and still not be a Christian. Then we said that the pupil is central; this was the emphasis of the public school. But this was inadequate, for if we center on the pupil, we contribute to the primeval sin, self-centeredness, human pride as over against God.

Today we say there are two centers in Christian education. It is not like a circle with one center, but it is an ellipse with two centers, two focuses. One of those centers is the person or the group, for it is true that we teach not so much facts or content as persons, with facts or content used to the end that the persons may be changed. The other center of the ellipse is God, the God who revealed himself in Jesus Christ. Now, to use an analogy from physics, these two centers, the person and God, are in tension. If that tension breaks, the relationship snaps. In the divine-human encounter, as man is confronted by his Maker, there is always tension.

Wherever there are two focuses there is a field of force. Where there is vitality, there is tension; there is a steady flow of energy between the two focuses: God and the person. Without tension there is lifelessness. When the field of force is dynamically charged, sparks are flying. You can feel something taking place.

Among the great moments in teaching are the occasions when you are conscious of the sparks flying, when you are aware of minds catching on fire or hearts becoming "strangely warm within" because of what God is doing. Such occasions do not occur without the aid of many a more pedestrian period. In Christian teaching you should make every effort to use the best content material available, to use all your knowledge of human personality, and to have the deepest possible concern and respect for every person in the class situation, including yourself.

The books on Christian education are just beginning to try to spell out what this means. Since 1950, Christian educators have suddenly and almost unanimously come to realize that subordinate emphases must give place to the divine-human encounter. Certainly we must recognize the importance of the person and the centrality of the Bible, but at its deepest, Christian education is concerned with the relationship and encounter between man and God. Martin Buber, a great Jewish philosopher, wrote a highly significant little book entitled *I and Thou* (Charles Scribner's Sons, rev. ed., 1958). The I-Thou relationship is, in its highest form, man in relationship with God, man encountering his Lord, and in its secondary form it refers to man in encounter with his fellow man, wherein one treats another not as an object to be used but as a person to be respected and related to in love.

This emphasis on encounter or relationship is not new. It is symbolized in the story of Jacob wrestling with the angel at Peniel (Gen. 32:24-32). God is not an abstract "It" to be talked about; he is a "Thou," a personal being to be related to in love and trust and holiness. Herein lies the fundamental difference between the philosophy of Christian education today and that prior to 1950. Beginning with the story in Gen., ch. 3, where God encountered Adam, asking, "Where are you?" and on through the Bible, the burden of the Book is of the various encounters between the Lord and his people. The creation story tells of the *imago Dei*—man created in the image of God. It means at least this, that man is made for fellowship with God. Seldom if ever does the Bible speak of God as an object to be discussed, but its theme is God and his mighty acts in regard to his people. Biblically, God is subject, not object. This living God who chose for himself a people was also related to Nineveh and Babylon. The New Testament reveals God the incarnate Son in his relationships with his disciples, the Pharisees, and others.

The purpose of Christian education is to have Christians confronted by their Lord. If evangelism is broadly interpreted, it is the same thing as this kind of Christian education. If Christian education is deeply and broadly interpreted, its aim is that of evangelism. Christian education normally has a more careful follow-through than has evangelism. One encounter with Christ in a lifetime is not enough. If a person is to grow, he grows by continual encounter. He grows by being rightly related, not just one day a week, but steadily and continuously, to his Maker. But this does not say everything. For when one is related to his Maker, he is also related to his fellow men. Jesus summarized the Law and the Prophets by saying: "You shall love the Lord your God with all your heart, and with all your soul, and with all your mind. . . . You shall love your neighbor as yourself" (Matt. 22:37, 39).

When we are confronted with God and won to him, we are changed within, and then we live the life of love toward our fellow men. Because God has loved us and we have accepted his love, we are able to love our fellow men and to love self. This is the philosophy of Christian education in ABC language. Christian education is about the vertical relation of God and man and the horizontal relationships of man with man. It is about love, the love of God and the love of self and the love of man. The Christian educator is concerned about the persons he teaches and their relationships with their Maker. In teaching, we try to bring about some deepening experience with God. This is our ultimate purpose which underlies and colors every class period. Knowledge is a means, a help, but the fundamental purpose is that our pupils and that we ourselves may come close to God in Christ, and in God's due time, may partake of "the measure of the stature of the fullness of Christ" (Eph. 4:13).

Around 1930 there was much talk of the goals of Christian education. The goals that became most famous were the ones developed by Paul Vieth in his doctoral study. The International Council of Religious Education, predecessor to the Division of Christian Education of the National Council of the Churches of Christ in the United States of America, adopted these goals and the participating denominations adapted them to their own frameworks. In the late 1950's there were restatements of goals in the youth division of the National Council of Churches, which are in a different category.

Most recently, some theorists have been saying that we have no right to set up goals at all. The very act of setting forth goals tends to make our work static rather than dynamic. Further, they insist that to be precise and specific in the statement of goals, at any level, is to make judgments which only God has a right to make. There is truth in what they are saying. To set up rigid and specific goals is to create the danger of a new Pharisaism. No teacher is wise enough to know exactly what God ought to do for a person or a class in a given teaching situation. This line of thought is an excellent corrective to legalistic or static attitudes, and to self-righteous priggishness. Nevertheless it is true that the wise teacher does have some aims, some goals, some purposes for his teaching program if not for each class session. And he tries so to teach that he meets the needs of his students. Certainly the new emphasis is correct in suggesting that our goals should be open-ended, recognizing on the one hand that new situations create new needs in persons, and on the other hand that the Holy Spirit will lead us each step of the way, showing us the goals as we need to know them.

Our definition of Christian education is as follows:

Christian education is the process of vital experiences by which the church and the family work together as nurturing communities to bring persons through Jesus Christ into right relations with God, self, man, and nature; and in which by reaching the whole person with the whole gospel, persons and groups are guided in such changes as enable them to grow steadily in these relationships, in dependence upon the power of the Holy Spirit.

How to Teach This Lesson

This lesson can probably best be taught by a combination of lecture and discussion, using such questions as:

- Why is Christian education important?
- What does Christian education mean to you?
- What goals do you think Christian education should have?
- Why are you considering becoming a teacher?
- What kind of Christian education did you receive as a child and youth?
- What is Christian maturity?

II

Communicating the Christian Faith in Our Era

The function of Christian education is to communicate the gospel. The gospel is unchanging, for Jesus Christ is the same yesterday and today and forever. The persons to whom and with whom we communicate, however, in some sense change considerably from generation to generation. In one sense man is always man—Homo sapiens—and his basic instincts, needs, desires, aspirations, hopes, dreams, and fears change not. Yet each man is the child of his own age and of his own culture. The gospel cannot possibly be communicated in the identical way today that was used in the first century or in the twelfth century. Effective communication requires an informed awareness of the nature of the society in which people live and an intelligent understanding of the mental and spiritual climate of the age. To teach the Christian religion to human beings in the second half of the twentieth century is not easy, for ours is an enormously complicated era. In some respects communication is far easier than it used to be, thanks to the media of mass communication—the radio, the television, the world press. There is a kind of common understanding abroad in the world. But that common understanding is not always an asset; the Christian thinker is likely to have ambivalent thoughts concerning the *Zeitgeist*—the spirit of the age. Let us look briefly at our era and at the things in it that make communication of the Christian gospel difficult.

First, the practical level. Two world wars in one generation have left us close to the edge of moral and spiritual bankruptcy. The professional optimist can always find some clue to suggest that people are steadily getting better. But it is elemental fact that after every great war there comes a moral letdown. We are not yet

21

out of that period. These two great wars, coming so close together, have helped to give the impression that human life is cheap. They have also given to many young people the foolish idea that "we had better have our fun and taste all the enticing experiences of life before it is too late." ("Let us eat, drink, and be merry, for tomorrow we die" is not merely an ancient Greek concept; it is the spiritual guideline of millions of moderns.)

To say "war" is to say "the bomb." *On the Beach* was, perhaps, exaggerated, but it is entirely likely that Western civilization, as we know it, would be almost entirely wiped out by an H-Bomb holocaust. Our only hope, humanly, is that we know this, and Russia knows this. But does China care? And so we live in the midst of this subtly terrifying uncertainty. Christianity, of course, has always known that the world would come to an end. But Christianity also has known that the world is not to be destroyed until God is ready for it to be destroyed (II Peter 3:11-13). Many moderns, knowing the possibilities, anesthetize themselves against reality in one way or another—liquor, drugs, play carried to Epicurean extremes, excessive speed, abnormal and incessant sex, compulsive busyness.

Much of the world, unfortunately, came to the conclusion that security is more to be desired than freedom. The totalitarian nation-state is no longer idolatrously promoted as it was by Hitler and Mussolini, but in subtle ways the concept is still with us. Those who equate "the American way of life" with "the Christian way" have trouble really hearing the gospel.

This is the era of mass man, not of man as a free individual, but of man herded into cities, rootless, restless, and anonymous. Mass man, working on the machine line, is not a person but a number. In the West, man is potential victim of automation, while in parts of Asia and in Africa man is leaping from primitive culture to the machine age in a brief span of time.

And mass man, if not herded into tenements, is likely to be stuffed into suburbs in tiny, poorly constructed look-alike houses. But even if the suburb be an upper-middle-class one, the mentality of the age is upon it, the age of conformity. "Keeping up with the Joneses" is no longer a silly expression; it is a way of life. Ours is a radar-directed culture. In some subcultures, notably that of high school youth, the antennae are out to catch each whispered current. We are the people who believe in conformity. This is the age of "togetherness." This is the era of "peace of mind." The "man in the gray-flannel suit" is part of "the lonely crowd," just another "organization man." He may go to church because everybody else does, but to communicate the gospel to him is not easy, for his real loyalties are to himself and his crowd, not to the Lord Jesus Christ, who calls men out of the world to be different. The typical suburbanite would be frightened by Paul's: "I appeal to you therefore, brethren, by the mercies of God, to present your bodies as a living sacrifice, holy and acceptable to God, which is your spiritual worship. Do not be conformed to this world but be transformed by the renewal of your mind, that you may prove what is the will of God, what is good and acceptable and perfect" (Rom. 12:1-2).

Now of course not all suburbanites are of this sort and not all city folk are anonymous. But this is our kind of world, and we had better recognize the fact. People who live under such conditions find it difficult to really listen to the gospel. They can hear the words, but to understand them is hard.

Second, the philosophical level. "When I look at thy heavens, . . . what is man?" (Ps. 8:3-4). The vast, illimitable spaces of heaven and the immensity of the starry universe overwhelm the human mind. When it is possible to speak of millions if not billions of suns, and to think in terms of millions of light-years, it is not easy to believe that man really has any significance. How can God care for an individual in a world so vast? In a world that has been here for two billion, possibly even six billion, years, how can we take the Genesis stories to be true? Is man, after all, just a cosmic accident, a "fortuitous conglomeration of atoms"? With the universe so vast and the world so old, is there a God who cares for me?

The philosophies that are dominant in our time are those which emphasize the physical, the material. Naturalism in one sophisticated form or another is widely held. Scientism is perhaps the most dangerous ism of our time, for it teaches that the only way to truth is through the use of the scientific method. Science is a wonderful instrument but a horrible master. If truth can be reached only through scientific experimentation of one sort or another, then revelation has no place and the Bible is a nice old relic.

Such philosophies as naturalism and scientism tend to deny the validity of the spiritual side of life, the reality of God, and the need for salvation. These philosophies have been held by the intelligentsia for a century or so. They have gradually seeped down to the average man who may try to be a religious person and yet a naturalist of some sort. Ours is what Sorokin called a "sensate age," one that finds its value in the senses. It is what Elton Trueblood called a "cut-flower civilization," for it is rootless. We are a materialistic people, for we are thing-minded. Now, people who emphasize the worth of things have difficulty in properly valuing persons or spirit. To say the least, Christian stewardship is meaningless to the materialist.

It was Nietzsche who regretted that God had died. Any number of people act as though God were dead. We live in a time of practical atheism. Practical atheists will not bother their minds with the question of God's existence but will live as they please. Many of them actually would affirm belief in God, but the belief seems to have little to do with their actions.

The existentialist writers have made us keenly aware of those who live bravely but despairingly. This is the only moment there is, and we will live it to the full—even if our hearts are empty, and we know that in the end life is meaningless. Life may be empty, but let us live bravely. "There is nothing new under the sun." (Eccl. 1:9.) The writer of Ecclesiastes said this long ago. "Vanity of vanities . . . . All is vanity." (Ch. 1:2.)

The world of modern thought is not unified. We have sciences, not science. We have multiversities, not universities. We have compartmentalized culture until professors in various departments can speak to one another only about the weather or the football team. And all this affects us as human beings—for we too are compartmentalized. Man, who should be rightly related to his God, his neighbors, and himself, is poorly related to all. He does not know who he is, he does not know how to get along with his fellows, and he is not on speaking terms with God.

In this world of alienation—from self, from neighbor, from God, from nature—man needs reconciliation and he needs it desperately, for without it he has no hope and he cannot love. In this world of alienation and hostility it is not easy for the gospel of reconciliation to be preached, taught, or lived. Yet this is our task!

Modern literature reveals man to us as being a secularist.

Robert H. Fitch, in a brilliant if controversial article on "Some Secular Images of Man in Contemporary Literature" *(Religious Education,* LIII, No. 2, March-April, 1958), says that a study of modern literature reveals man to be complacent, despairing, defiant, living in an ecstasy of anguish. The plays of Tennessee Williams, seen by millions on the screen and read by thousands, reveal persons who are sometimes pathetic but more often "basically obscene." Fitch suggests that for these characters the ends of life are sex and money. The French writer Camus had a more deeply perceptive touch perhaps, but he was at best a noble agnostic. In his novels man is brave yet weak, and sinner without divine grace. The Beatniks are a contemporary witness to our jaded civilization. Perhaps teen-agers can understand "cool, man, cool," and "flip the scene," and most of us may guess at the meaning of "'way out," but how can a generation that constantly addresses persons as "Daddy-o" really grasp the glory of divine Fatherhood?

Although in many a church there are lots of people who are but little affected by modern philosophies, all are more affected than they realize by the practical aspects of modern living. To be specific, look at the matter of mobility. Twenty per cent of our people move each year. Thousands of children do not go two years to the same church or the same school. Roots are not sunk deeply into the life of the community. Highly mobile people are not likely to learn the deeper meanings of the ways and spirit and beliefs of a community. That makes communication more difficult at all the more important levels.

Certainly most of our church people still believe in God and the reality of the spiritual. But to unfold the meaning of the gospel to them is more difficult by far today than in some earlier generations. The language of Zion is not their native language; they have to learn it! Our task as Christian educators is to communicate the gospel to folk who live in the space age.

Communicating the Christian Faith

What, then, is communication? It is saying what you mean in such a way as to be understood by the person or persons to whom you are talking. Effective communication includes being understood by others as saying what you really say, not something almost like what you said. And you say what you say not simply by words, but by emotional tone, by spirit, by quality of life.

Such communication is not easy on any subject. It is notably difficult in the sphere of religion. The man who thinks it is easy to talk to modern people about Christianity is pitifully naïve. It is easy to talk about any subject in which one is interested, but it is not easy to talk effectively in order to communicate to others what you are really saying.

What is it that makes communication difficult? In general, the meaning of the words. A given word does not mean precisely the same thing to any two individuals. Take a simple word such as "food." To all men, whatever the language, food means that which eases one's hunger. But the word has ramifications. Food to a Cantonese is apt to suggest rice; to a Texas rancher, sirloin steak; to an Italian, spaghetti; to a slum dweller, cabbage; to a teen-ager, Cokes and hamburgers. The emotional overtones of the word "food" are different for the permanently hungry Indian peasant and the perennially full American.

In short, the meaning of a word differs according to the experiences we have had with that particular word or phrase. The one word "Shakespeare" conjures up for the collegian memories of English 401—of *Hamlet* and *Macbeth* and *As You Like It*. But the word may be totally meaningless to an illiterate. To the man of culture, the word "Rachmaninoff" speaks of music, but to the man on the street it sounds like the name of the fullback for Villanova, or perhaps the offensive left tackle at Notre Dame. (Here the writing team differs in interpreting the word "offensive"!) On Lincoln's birthday a certain newspaper came out with a story, allegedly true, of the six-year-old who came home from Sunday school to say that the teacher had talked about Abraham, but that she did not seem to know that Abraham's last name was Lincoln!

Take such common words as "faith," "hope," "love," "courage," "duty"—how manifold are their variations in meaning! "Love," specifically, to one means lust; to another, "walking on pink and blue clouds"; to another, a mother tenderly caring for a little one; to another, an aged couple sharing the last years of life in simplicity; to another, "going steady"; to another, "a diamond"; to another, "brotherly love"; to another, John 3:16; to another, the *agapē* of God pouring into the human heart and being released in *agapē* to mankind.

The meaning of words varies with our experiences. In fact, the meaning of a given word to a given individual may change considerably as the years pass. The child's concept of God traditionally has been that of a huge old man with a long white beard. The time may come when the child, now man, thinks of God as the Eternal Spirit who is both Creator and Redeemer and who is best known to us as we see him incarnate in Jesus Christ. Ah—but likewise the time may come when the term "God" is just part of a curse word or an outmoded and needless assumption of poor ignorant little people.

The meaning of a word varies with the era in which it is used. When the Revised Standard Version was being published, we learned afresh how greatly words had changed since the King James Version was first published back in 1611. Such words as "prevent," "virtue," "suffer," and "carriage" have totally changed meaning. But we don't have to go that far back. The word "atom" to the average high school student in 1925 was a perfectly familiar word that he had to master in order to pass chemistry or physics. That same word today has terrifying connotations, for man has learned the secret of the atom to use for universal good or universal destruction, and the choice is in the balances.

Sometimes words that are perfectly clear when they are separate become difficult to grasp when they are put together as an idea. Practically every word that the philosopher Whitehead uses is a familiar English word, but one reads Whitehead quite slowly with a dictionary at hand to trace the subtle shades of meaning. So with Sören Kierkegaard or Karl Barth or Paul Tillich.

It has been said, and truly, that the average congregation today no longer knows "the language of Zion"; that, in short, if a preacher uses Biblical references that were perfectly familiar to his grandfathers, the probability is that in his own congregation today there will be many to whom the reference is as meaningless as would be a reference to an obscure passage in Augustine or Irenaeus. Once, young seminary students were taught that the best possible illustrations were to be found in the Bible. Today seminary students are taught that while Biblical illustrations are still the best, one has to master the art of using them without taking half the sermon to explain the illustration.

We have known for sixty years that graded lessons are absolutely essential if we really want to teach people of different ages. Ages differ in their understanding of history and of theology. It takes no genius to realize that the average three-year-old cannot understand the doctrine of the atonement. What is harder to grasp is that the average layman has all too slight an understanding of the doctrine, and the average minister is hard pressed to show anything like a profound grasp of that which the wisest men know to be the greatest of mysteries. Abstract theological concepts from the pulpit or in the classroom are to most folk, regardless of age, boring and meaningless. The vocabulary of the professional theologian—justification, sanctification, prevenient grace—must be translated into language "understanded of the common people" if it is to be of value. These very sentences reveal the difficulty of communication, for the authors believe worth-while religious communication will inevitably have theological and Biblical rootage.

We have learned of late that Christian thinkers must take their own language more seriously. Every special aspect of culture has its own peculiar vocabulary, and the man who specializes in a given aspect of culture has to learn its vocabulary. The baseball world has its own verbal symbols; so does the medical world. The astrophysicists use symbols too intricate for most of us, and lawyers can becloud the meaning of any sentence through the use of legal terms. It is unadulterated nonsense to think that theology can do without a special vocabulary. The men who do the basic thinking in the realm of religion will always be men who can and do have a firm understanding of the world of Biblical and theological symbols. The average Christian and the average church school teacher will never be masters of the verbal symbols of the Christian faith. They should, however, have an elementary acquaintance with the basic words. A technical word like "supralapsarianism" is for the technical scholar, but every Christian ought to know the meaning of such terms as creation and fall, law and gospel, grace and peace, guilt and temptation. Every mature Christian also needs to understand such Biblical-theological truths as election, justification by faith, and divine sovereignty. Christian education must give people tools to work with in the form of words and concepts as well as stories and facts. We cannot think Christianly without knowing the Christian words. Christian life roots in Christian doctrine. Jesus Christ is personally the Truth, and grace and love and faith and hope and judgment are truths that take their meaning from him. Such truths must take on meaning through encounter and through teaching.

For the first time in the history of Western culture, we have reached a state wherein millions of people do not really know what the minister is talking about when he uses such simple words as "God," "eternal life," "prayer," "salvation," "grace." They are words that can be looked up in the dictionary, but they do not get across to millions. "The joy of salvation" is a phrase that can be voiced in many a business office or factory without eliciting one single glimmer of understanding. Ours is a sensate civilization; ours is an era that believes in things but not in Spirit. Of course statistically one can prove that the churches are growing, that over 50 per cent of the populace has church membership. But statistics do not tell the whole truth, and in fact, in this case largely conceal the real truth, which is that to communicate the deep things of the Spirit is extraordinarily difficult in an age wherein men have deserted Almighty God to follow some ism—communism or nationalism or naturalism or humanism. In the age of mass man, how can the individual worker see beyond his place as a cog in the machine to his place as a child of God? In these days of the reign of scientism, how can the pupil in the classroom realize that alongside of the road of scientific method that leads to truth there is another road, less easy to see, but that reaches the goal even more surely, the road of faith?

Granted, then, that the new science of semantics has its place, granted that we live in an age wherein vast hordes of people are simply indifferent to the things that are spiritually discerned, how can we most effectively communicate the Christian gospel to the modern man who values success more than he values salvation?

What Happens in Real Communication?

To communicate the Christian faith is to give from our life and spirit into the life and spirit of others an understanding of what the Christian faith really means to us *on the inside*. Such communication is difficult. We say what we say not simply by words, but also by emotional tone, by spirit, by quality of life. The church has a gospel to communicate, a deed to proclaim, a revelation from God of his saving act in Jesus Christ, and the church also has a faith to communicate; we want not only to tell others

of the Christian faith but also to show them our personal attitude
of faith in him. The gospel we communicate is communicated to
and with this strange being called man, whose true nature is seen
in Jesus Christ but whose defiled nature is all too evident, and
this very sinfulness makes communication more difficult. Communication occurs in community, not in isolation. While individual may communicate to individual, the Christian faith is communicated by the Christian community and in the Christian
community—the Christian family, the Christian church, and the
Christian small group. The center of our teaching, therefore, is to
be found in the effort to make real the divine-human encounter,
to help our pupils to have a dynamic confrontation with God in
Christ. Out of such meeting of Spirit with spirit comes the Christian life.

Now, how does it all come about? How does communication
take place? The communication of the Christian faith in the
objective or in the subjective sense takes place in the light of such
considerations as have been suggested in the preceding paragraph.

Some of what is to follow may seem to be a bit abstract, but it is
very real. Let us therefore be quite concrete at this point and say:

—to communicate the Christian faith involves using words that
are understood by those to whom one speaks;
—to communicate the Christian faith involves trying to live up
to the words one utters;
—to communicate the Christian faith involves using the best
available tools—quarterlies, books, audio-visuals;
—to communicate the Christian faith involves using the best
teaching techniques based upon our knowledge of how people
learn;
—to communicate the Christian faith involves using the best
possible teachers, of whom the parents are pre-eminently first.
This in turn involves a steady and an intelligent program for
the education of leaders;
—to communicate the gospel effectively through the church
school involves selecting the best possible teachers, training
them to be effective teachers, and guiding these workers as
they endeavor to engage in Christian education;
—to communicate the Christian faith effectively through the
life of the church involves a serious effort to have a genuine
fellowship—in the rich Christian usage of the word;

—to communicate the Christian faith is impossible unless one who would communicate believes that faith because one's faith in Jesus Christ is genuine.

Effective communication involves yet other matters. But let us now move into the question of what actually takes place when a human being is taught Christian truth. How do I learn what it means to be a Christian? How can I grow in Christlikeness? How can I have the kind of relationship with God in Christ that will make me a new creation who lives the life of love? How can I know God?

In the preceding paragraph we have suggested some of the human means to such goals. Categorically, I learn Christian truth as any other religious truth is learned, through good teaching by good people. I use my mind. I think. I reason. I meditate. I act. And at last I understand. And yet this is not the whole story. The matter is not this simple. When I have used my mind to the full, when good Christian folk have used the best possible teaching methods, then I can have a mental knowledge of the phrases used by Christians when they talk about their religion. But while there is a sense in which I may discover Christian truth, there is a deeper sense in which I cannot discover the meaning of Christ, or the inner meaning of the word "God." For lo! what I had thought was discovery actually turns out to be revelation. Man seeks. God reveals. Seldom does God reveal unless man is seeking, and yet again, the priority is always with God. The ancient doctrine of prevenient grace is true in Christian teaching as it is in the realm of salvation. God moves first. "But God shows his love for us in that while we were yet sinners Christ died for us." (Rom. 5:8.)

It is possible to find folk who think that the only essential in a Christian teacher is a profoundly spiritual life with God. This does have top priority, but it is not enough. Christian teaching calls for people to use the best possible educational methods, to have the best possible educational tools, to use their minds to the full and to endeavor to stimulate their pupils to use their minds too. Those who teach the Christian religion, at home or in church school, should themselves be taught, should learn to use the best educational methods known to man, and should dare to think fearlessly about all aspects of the faith.

The human discovery of the meaning of God and Christ is always preceded by the divine self-revelation. It is possible for us to know God only because God gives himself in Christ to us. And he does so in and through the Christian community, not in a vacuum.

Frequently we hear it said that religion is caught, not taught. This is a catchy and cute half-truth. Of course a parent does not teach a child, "I love you, my child," simply by repeating the words ten times a day. And of course religion is not taught in any mechanical rote fashion. Just as the child comes to understand that his parents love him by the total tenor of the parents' lives, attitudes, and actions, far more than by their words, so does a person learn religious truth from the life, attitudes, and actions of the teacher far more than from his words. But the point is, *that is teaching*. A human child learns, not merely by absorption, but rather by an active grasping. The human child is not a bit of plastic stuff that can be molded with absolute ease; rather, the child is a dynamic being who makes some contribution to his own growth. Any parent who listens thoughtfully to the conversation and play talk of his child when the child is unaware of adult observation will soon realize that the child is actively and even aggressively trying out words and ideas for size. When religious truth is presented to me, I do not merely absorb it, I actually grasp it. That is, I reach out for it and take it and make it my own. Religious communication is a two-way street. A religious truth, idea, concept, experience, or, more deeply, a religious relationship, is not simply a matter of a teacher talking about the thing, but also it is a matter of the pupil reaching out actively to take hold of the thing.

In short, there is no communication in the realm of spiritual values unless both the one who is endeavoring to communicate and the one to whom he is trying to communicate set up a two-way conversation. This two-way conversation does not have to be with words, but I can't teach you if you simply aren't interested, whereas I can teach you easily if you actively reach out to grasp my communication to you. You can lead a horse to water, but you can't make him drink. You cannot teach another a spiritual truth or give another a great spiritual experience against his will. Yet, "whosoever will may may come." You can successfully communicate to me whenever I show real interest in what you are trying to say, whenever I act upon your word, whenever I for myself try out the truth which you enunciate, or better, which you live. This, of course, is why communication in religious matters is always hard. Even if you hear my words with your mind, I have not succeeded in communicating to you until you also hear them with your heart.

There is yet a deeper principle. Obedience is in order to knowledge. "Trust and obey, for there's no other way To be happy with Jesus, But to trust and obey." Those words are neither great poetry nor great music, but they half hide and half reveal a great truth. Obedience is the organ of spiritual knowledge. "If you continue in my word, you are truly my disciples, and you will know the truth, and the truth will make you free." (John 8:31-32.) If you love me, keep my commandments, and you shall know; so speaks Jesus in the upper room. (John, chs. 13 to 17.) And so we are back at the ellipse with its two focuses. The heart of Christian teaching is in the relationship between God and man. Our goal always is to bring man into the right relationship with God through Christ. "Obey me, and you will understand what I say, yes, you will know the truth, and the truth will make you free." But what is this truth? It is not a matter of knowledge or of facts; it is a matter of a saving act—I am the truth, says Jesus of himself (John 14:6), and the truth that sets one free is Jesus in action redeeming men. Now if obedience is the key to spiritual knowledge, Christian teaching cannot be a mere pouring of knowledge into empty minds, but it is ever and always an effort to bring human beings into a relationship of trust that leads to obedience and so to knowledge. "Ah, Christ, I cannot know thee, for I have never seen thee." So we are prone to say, and yet down the ages comes the refrain, "I am the life, try me out, live by me, and you shall know life eternal." Christian teaching is the effort so to bring our pupils into a relationship with Jesus that with the fullness of that human freedom implied by the words *imago Dei,* they will yield themselves in loving trust and humble obedience to Jesus Christ as the Lord of Life. In tension we live—always in tension, the human over against the divine, with the air electric between them. And yet in that relationship there is the *agapē* of God, the "John 3:16 love" of God, and the replying faith of man, which therefore receives the love of God into its inner nature and so is able to show that love unto itself and its neighbors. I-Thou!

Last, but not least, as we consider what happens in real communication of the Christian gospel, is the fact of the Holy Spirit. The Holy Spirit is, in ABC language, the living God at work in the hearts of men now. His home is the church, but like the wind he is not limited as to when and where and how he works. It is customary for overly pious Christians to talk too much about the Holy Spirit, whereas average Christians and the younger generation tend to speak and think too seldom of the Holy Spirit. Actually, it is in and by the Spirit that we Christians live. By him we are called into the Christian faith, and into the Christian family; by him we are enabled to grow in grace; by him is the church sustained; by him is the ministry of Word and sacraments a channel of blessing. Yes! And by him is Christian education possible. In the last analysis, there is no successful communication without the work of the Holy Spirit. *Man must do all he can, yet without the aid of the Holy Spirit our teaching is in vain.*

And how does the Holy Spirit enter the educational process? In the end, it is a mystery. Yet, humanly, we can at least begin to understand. He is in the learner, to help him to want to learn, to reach out actively to grasp that which is being communicated. He is in the teacher, to give him "words of wisdom," "the right word at the proper moment," the flash of insight that opens up a new way, the inner faith by which he lives. And he is in the relationship between teacher and learner. The atmosphere of the teaching process is charged with the power of the Holy Spirit. And in that tension which the Holy Spirit creates between teacher and learners, the Christian faith is grasped, the divine-human encounter becomes a glorious reality, the pupil comes to know Christ, and so to love himself and his fellows in Christ. In that kind of tension, the person grows in Christ. Just as all real living is meeting, so is all teaching—and this, in the Holy Spirit! and not without deep faith and unceasing prayer.

To communicate the Christian gospel is, therefore, not merely a technique; it is an art also, and more deeply, a life so wholly committed to the Lord that his Spirit in us somehow speaks to the spirits of those to whom we would communicate. We can communicate only as they are not hes, shes, or its, but thous in an I-Thou relationship that is based upon and grows out of this primal I-Thou relationship with the Lord of Life.

How to Teach This Lesson

This lesson could easily be expanded to several sessions. The chief characteristics of our era could be discussed at length through a process of research groups and reports. One person, for instance, could report on what we learn from the current writers of novels and plays concerning communication, while another could report on why communication on religious subjects is made more difficult by the hidden presupposition of our time that the only real truth is by way of science. The material in the book gives some clues along these lines. Specific suggestions:

1. Role-play a situation in which two leaders call on a typical American humanist family and try to talk to them about the Christian faith, only to find they have no common language. Husband and wife keep asking, "What do you mean by that?" or they may say, "But I haven't the faintest idea what you mean." One of the visitors should be sensitive to the situation; the other has a facile tongue and uses all the Christian words easily, perhaps too easily.

2. Divide the class into buzz groups to discuss for a few minutes the statement, "What the parents in our church need to do is to discipline their children." Select the reporters beforehand and secretly ask them to pay particular attention to the varying interpretations of the word "discipline." These differences should be reported to the entire group.

3. Discuss: How mass communication has changed the world views of people; or discuss: How audio-visuals have changed the teaching process in our time.

4. Research: Have your class members ask ten persons each to define a list of ten common Christian words, such as "forgiveness," "grace," "sin," "holy," "atonement," "justice," "good," etc.

5. Have a general discussion on the question, Can the gospel be communicated today in the identical ways that were used in the first century?

III

The Church, the Fellowship of Learners

The church, as the covenant community, is the beloved fellowship of learners, in which the people of God, together with their children, worship and witness. It teaches by its life, and all who are members are disciples for life.

Informed people no longer conceive of Christian education as being limited to the Sunday school. Thirty years ago there was too sharp a separation between the church and the Sunday school, which often was considered a separate institution. Now we know that the Sunday church school is the church at work teaching, or more accurately, it is the formal organization of the church for its teaching work.

Communication occurs in community; the church is a nurturing community. While the family is the primary community of Christian nurture, the church is the secondary community that supplements the nurturing work of the family, and for some families it has to do all the work of Christian education. The church educates, or it does not live. One of the best descriptions of the church is as the fellowship of learning. One major denomination is now constructing a new curriculum around the concept of the church as the covenant community. In the body of which Christ is the head, its members learn of him, for Christians are lifelong disciples. Christian education is from womb to tomb; in a real sense it begins when prospective parents begin to pray for their unborn child, and it continues as long as life lasts. First in the context of the family and then in the context of the church, the child receives Christian nurture.

The essence of Christian education is the fact of relationship, divine and human. By virtue of the relationships in the body of

Christ, believers are enabled to grow in faith and in the courage and wisdom to live as Christians in the midst of a pagan and perverse generation. Adults have their relationships with the church as full-fledged members, and as such their relationships with their fellow members are in theory mature in quality. In actual fact, the quality of the relationships between church members varies considerably with the churches and the members. "Behold how these Christians love one another!" was an ancient comment on how and why the church grew so rapidly. On the whole, in our relationships in the church, we grow in faith and love. As Lewis Sherrill pointed out in his great book, *The Gift of Power* (The Macmillan Company, 1955; p. 45): "The self is formed in its relationships with others. If it becomes deformed, it becomes so in its relationships. If it is reformed or transformed, that too will be in its relationships."

A community has been defined as "a body of relationships which affect the becoming of its individual members." The church is a genuine community, composed of humans who are related to one another in organized fashion.

Among its characteristics are: (1) A sense of being together, a feeling of like-mindedness—akin to but deeper than the adolescent's "The more we get together the happier we'll be." (And surely more profound than the Madison Avenue image of "togetherness.") (2) Bearing one another's burdens. John Calvin, commenting on the Lord's Supper, said that when one prays, "Our Father . . ." he has in effect acknowledged all men to be his brothers and that they have a claim upon him for what they need. (*Institutes of the Christian Religion*, III. xx. 37; The Westminster Press, 1960). Paul discussing the church makes it clear that each part of the body has need of each other part, "As it is, there are many parts, yet one body" (I Cor. 12:20). (3) All members treating one another as persons—and where this is not done, the community is sick. The unfortunate happenings in the Congo following its liberation are partially explained in the profound and pathetic prayer of a fine Christian pastor, Isaac Kanyinda, on June 30, 1960, "We praise thee that this day we have officially joined the race of humanity." (4) Each member having his own particular contribution to make to the whole; and therefore having some feeling of significance. (See I Cor. 12:12-26.)

"Here [in the church] there cannot be Greek and Jew, circum-

cised and uncircumcised, barbarian, Scythian, slave, free man, but
Christ is all, and in all." (Col. 3:11.) For, "There is neither Jew
nor Greek, there is neither slave nor free, there is neither male
nor female; for you are all one in Christ Jesus." (Gal. 3:28.) The
Christian community is heterogeneous in that it should be composed of all sorts of persons from all sorts of backgrounds, though
it is homogeneous in the sense that its members are all one in
Jesus Christ. The Christian society must contain "unlikes as well
as likes." There are and there ought to be tensions within the
church, the tensions that grow out of different backgrounds and
different approaches to the common center. Where there is no
such tension there is no true life. Creative interaction between
various kinds of people is essential for the well-being of the
church. In the Christian church the qualifications for membership
have no relationship to skin color or social status or size of bank
account. In particular churches that are strictly homogeneous
there is always a lack of dynamic tension and therefore always a
strong tendency to be self-satisfied.

In the church the members are set in a great historical succes-
sion. We are reminded of the beautiful statement of Lewis Sherrill: "Spiritually no one ever enters the sanctuary alone" (*op. cit.*,
p. 53). The anonymous author of Hebrews said it long ago:
"Therefore, since we are surrounded by so great a cloud of wit-
nesses . . ." (ch. 12:1). We have a common Scripture, a common history, a communion liturgy some of whose phrases, if not sentences,
go back to the early part of the second century—a common heritage—which we all should know.

The Christian community is a fellowship of the Holy Spirit, so
that God's power is ever available to those who are open to it
and are seeking it. L. S. Thornton in his great book, *The Common Life in the Body of Christ* (p. 4; The Dacre Press, London,
2d ed., 1944), reminds us that this common life is "participation
in the life of God through union with the one man Jesus Christ"
(Rom. 5:15). "But the essence of the ecclesia is a mutual sharing
in the grace of our Lord Jesus Christ, the love of God and the gift
of the Holy Spirit." (*Ibid.*, p. 92.) "The unity of the body is a living unity created and sustained by the one Spirit." (*Ibid.*, p. 94.)
If these words from a powerful Anglo-Catholic thinker seem too
mystical, listen to John Calvin: "But all the elect are so united in
Christ that as they are dependent on one Head, they also grow

together into one body, being joined and knit together as are the limbs of a body. They are made truly one since they live together in one faith, hope, and love, and in the same Spirit of God. For they have been called not only into the same inheritance of eternal life but also to participate in one God and Christ." (*Institutes of the Christian Religion,* IV. i. 2; The Westminster Press, 1960). In its deepest sense, the church's life comes through Jesus Christ. One does not have to be a mystic to grasp that fact. The Edinburgh Conference on Faith and Order said in 1937, "It is the body of Christ, whose members derive their life and oneness from the one living Head; and thus it is nothing apart from him but is in all things dependent upon the power of salvation which God has committed to his Son." This divine-human nature of the church is not like Oriental mysticism which leads to the identity of man with God or rather the loss of man's personality in the Absolute. The mystical unity of the church with its Lord is like that in Gal. 2:20 in which Paul says: "I live; yet not I, but Christ liveth in me" (KJV). This is unity, but it is not identity.

The church is the covenant community. It is the inheritor of the promises of God to the people of Israel. Someone has said that the covenant calls into being the redeemed family of God. The church is the people of God, called apart from the world in order to serve him by bearing testimony of his grace and his goodness to the world. Election is to service rather than merely to privilege. Most Christians believe that this covenant is for believers and their children, so they practice infant baptism. Presbyterians, Episcopalians, Lutherans, Roman Catholics, Greek Catholics, and Methodists are the major denominational families that so interpret the Bible.

Election is for service and the covenant people are chosen, not because they are especially deserving nor that they should have whereof to glory, but that in and through them God would have a nurturing, redemptive community with which to bear witness of his mighty deeds for the salvation of the world. The church is both witness to the grace of God in Jesus Christ and instrument of God for the salvation of the world. (The curriculum study materials of the Presbyterian Church U.S. have pointed up the words "witness" and "instrument.")

As has been intimated, the church is the body of Christ, a divine-human organism, not just another human organization.

The New Testament metaphors of the church, such as body, temple, vine, bride, all point to organization but something that is not mere organization. "Organism" is the better word. The church is the living organism of which Christ is the heart, the animating principle, and it lives only as his lifeblood flows through its veins, cleansing, nourishing, and continually renewing it.

The church is self-transcending; it gets above and beyond its structural details and its pathetic frailties. The church is divine; it lives in Christ.

But the church is human too. It contains within it persons such as you and me, folk who are frail, weak, sometimes selfish, sometimes blind, sometimes rebellious, who know but refuse to do their Master's will. "The Christian church as we know it, is divided, worldly, stupid, corrupt, apathetic, stuffy, and at the same time it is the bride of Christ, his sacred body. The church is not the body of Christ because her members are good or wise or even nice, but because she believes in Christ, and he is her true and hidden life." (Nathaniel Micklem, *What Is Faith?* pp. 218-219; Cokesbury Press, 1937.) There is in the church what Sherrill called a "splitness." Not all of the life of the fellowship is genuine, not all of its life is *koinōnia,* mutual participation in the life of the body. The church is composed of people called saints, not because they are peculiarly holy morally but because they are set apart for God. The church is composed of forgiven sinners on the way to salvation, not of perfected saints. Its life, therefore, is not all harmony and peace and brotherly love. Sometimes its members affect one another negatively or harshly. Sometimes its members let the old man of sin get the upper hand temporarily even in the life of the church. This institution, the church, so divine yet so human, is both a wonderful and yet a dangerous place in which to attempt Christian education.

The Notes of the Church

As we look at the church, we see that it has some clear-cut functions or purposes. Every particular church in a local community endeavors to fulfill these functions. Men state these notes differently, but the books on the church come out with approximately the same concepts of what the functions of the church are.

The first note is worship. The church exists to worship God.

"Man's chief end is to glorify God and to enjoy him forever."
Worship is the highest activity of any society, and the church is
the one society in the world that is specifically and particularly
united in order to worship God. Worship is our response in faith
within the community to the grace of God. Through worship we
renew our relationships with our Heavenly Father in loving trust
and simple faith. The cynic and the organization man alike tend
to downgrade corporate worship. But the most faithful members
of the church are those who are most certain that in common worship they receive strength and guidance for the pilgrimage of life.
Children, too, learn to worship by worshiping, both within the
family circle and in the family pew. In common worship, not the
preacher, not the choir, not the architecture, but GOD is central,
and to him all turn for renewal. This I-Thou relationship is the
basic one of life, and it can never be simply an individual relationship of one man and God. The individual believer inevitably becomes a part of the Christian fellowship, and his worship must
be corporate as well as personal.

The second mark of the church is concern, love, *koinōnia*.
Loving Christ so much, we must love the brethren. The church
is that body or that community wherein the spirit of love reigns.
In it there is genuine concern one for the other; in it there is a
bearing of one another's burdens. The phrase, the communion of
saints, excellently expresses what the church ought to be. The life
of the church can and should meet our fundamental needs of love,
acceptance, forgiveness, and common devotion to a cause. Only
God can fully meet our needs, however, and the church partakes
too much of our common humanity ever fully to meet our needs.
Yet the basic spiritual needs of mankind can be met in the church
more simply and more intimately and more effectively than in
any other community besides the family, and even the family must
turn to the church for its inspiration and guidance. In Christian
education we teach people to love one another. Sometimes the
life of the congregation tends to deny what we teach. If a church
teaches that God loves everybody and then has unacknowledged
but very real membership requirements that effectively bar some
humans, some thoughtful persons may wonder whether hypocrisy
or love is the dominant note of Christian living.

The third note is witness, evangelism, a missionary concern for
the salvation of all men. Where this note is lacking the church is

dying. If we must teach to live, it is also true that the living church is lovingly and passionately evangelistic in its concern for the least, the lowest, and the lost among men. This concern extends to all men everywhere. "To the end of the world and the ends of the earth," is Lesslie Newbigin's apt phrase in *The House-hold of God* (Friendship Press, 1953; p. xli).

Recently we have realized anew that mutual concern which expresses itself in pastoral care of the church for its members is an essential part of the life of the church. "Each member of the body is to be concerned for each other member, and for the whole." The priesthood of believers was intended to lead to "the mutual care of souls on the part of laymen." John T. McNeill, in his valuable book *A History of the Cure of Souls* (Harper & Brothers, 1951; p. 190), aptly phrased it, "the care of all for the souls of all." In a Christian group, there ought to be a loving concern for each member. The church we know best has endeavored to put this principle into operation. In times of illness and death and tragedy and suffering, the congregation ministers to these people as does the minister. One of the writers can bear testimony to the reality of the pastoral concern of lay members of the church. Some phases of pastoral care and counseling only a trained clergyman can carry out, but a significant trend in the church of tomorrow will be the emphasis on the laity taking over much of the work of pastoral care.

The final note, which will be discussed at some length, is *nurture*. Before discussing that main topic, we desire to call attention to other ways of looking at the church. The Reformers defined the marks of the true church as the pure preaching of the Word of God; the administration of the sacraments according to Christ's ordinance; and church discipline.

The church is one, holy, apostolic, and catholic. These familiar creedal words are of utmost significance. The church is *one*. One in Christ. The oneness refers primarily to spiritual unity rather than to organizational uniformity. This unity in Christ already exists but needs to be expressed. John, ch. 17, with its "that they may all be one; . . . that the world may believe . . ." reminds us that in some profound sense there can only be one church just as there is one Lord. This is not to be thought of as a literalistic "one-churchism," but ultimately the unity of the church must have visible form.

The church is *holy*. It is indwelt and controlled by the Holy Spirit and its members are called to a life of holiness. Its members are not literally holy but are in process of becoming what God intends for them to be.

The church is *catholic*. That is, ecumenical or universal. Its message is for all men in all ages all over the world. And that message has the catholicity of truth. All Christians and all Christian denominations belong to the holy catholic church and it is a deep shame that Rome, which is one of the sects of the church, has been accorded almost sole possession of this mark of the church. There is a Roman branch of the catholic church, an Orthodox branch, a Lutheran branch, a Methodist branch, a Presbyterian branch, a Congregationalist branch, and so on.

The church is *apostolic*. There is a genuine continuity between the church of today and the church to which the apostles ministered. The inner life of the church today is continuous with the inner life of the church of the apostles' day. The church of today has the same message, the same gospel, the same Lord, the same spirit of love flowing from God's Spirit. The church has received by divine gift the Word, the sacraments, and the ministry; all of which are apostolic in origin and in nature. The gift of Christ to his church, they came first to the handful of apostles and disciples and so to us today. Further, the church is apostolic in that the word means "sent on a mission," and the church is surely sent on a mission to the world of our time. The apostolicity of the church is its mission.

One of the primary means by which the church seeks to fulfill its mission is Christian education. That congregation which is carrying out its work effectively is bound to have a program of Christian education. Obviously education goes along with worship and fellowship and evangelism; each function is supported by and interacts with each other function. Three or four simple propositions will set forth the teaching function of the church.

First, the whole church teaches by its whole life. The common life of the body teaches. In other words, teaching in the church is not limited to the sermons of the preacher, or to the Sunday church school classes. If the teachers are doing their task well, they will teach not only facts but attitudes and will help to bring about the right relationships with God and man that are so important in Christian living. The church teaches by everything that it is and does. A nurturing community is not simply a school where one goes for so many hours and then departs, hoping something has been learned. The nurturing community is a community where people are together, working together, praying together, thinking together, affecting one another in multiform ways, relating to one another. The church teaches, so Howard Grimes words it, "more by what it does than by what it says, and even more by what it is than what it does" (*The Church Redemptive*, p. 91; Abingdon Press, 1958). The church, then, teaches by its worship, which may be reverent and sincere, or which may be overly casual, poorly prepared, not taken seriously. The church teaches by the attitudes of its deacons toward the church property and the use of the church. If the deacons are more concerned with the care and preservation of a piece of furniture than they are with the growth and vitality and enthusiasm of twelve-year-olds, they teach that property is more important than persons.

No one should encourage disorderly conduct or gross mistreatment of church property, but it is far better for church equipment to wear out a few years sooner, than it is for church children to be driven from the church by "the society for the preservation of church furnishings." The church teaches by its missionary outlook. Is it concerned and informed only about its little place in the Lord's vineyard, or is it concerned with the gospel for all men everywhere? The church teaches by what things it values most, by what it spends its money on—for splash and show or for sound education, for ever more costly furnishings or for a larger benevolence budget, for paying off the debt more quickly or for adequate salaries for its employees, and for the minister. The church teaches by the peace or the strife of its members as they work together in its ongoing program. The church teaches by what the children sense the adults feel toward one another. The church teaches by the comments made at the dinner tables on Sunday. In short, the church teaches primarily by what its members are and how they live as a church, and only secondarily by its formal educational program.

In any kind of community, the adults cannot escape being teachers. If you are an adult, you are a teacher. If you are a church member, you are a teacher. (Even "a little child shall lead them.") Somebody sees you; somebody observes you. Whether or not you say a word, they will sense your attitudes and your spirit.

This is particularly true in the Christian community.

What, however, do we teach? Do we teach *agapē*—self-giving love, the kind that "seeks not her own, is not easily provoked," but is constantly giving, or do we teach something quite different? What are the social attitudes we impart?

Howard Grimes brilliantly suggests, "The curriculum is . . . what the person takes home with him" (*op. cit.*, p. 103). Curriculum is not just what the Sunday church school teacher has tried to teach, nor is it the set of facts given; it is also attitudes, atmosphere, and spirit picked up in the living church. The facts learned are important but ancillary to the relationships established and developed. The whole church is a school, and it teaches by all that it is. But the educational function of the church, as we have seen, is not its only function.

Secondly, in most denominations the official board is responsible for the life and teaching of the congregation. In the Presbyterian Church, for instance, the governing body, the session, has general control of the life of the church and all its subsidiary agencies such as the Sunday church school, the men's and women's organizations of the church, and the youth groups. In a large church, the governing body will normally set apart a committee on Christian education and will delegate to that committee certain clear-cut responsibilities and duties. The Christian education committee is responsible to the session or other governing body. It sets policies and principles of action and is charged with securing and training adequate personnel to carry out the necessary leadership functions. The staff of teachers is under the administrative oversight of the church school superintendent.

Thirdly, the minister is primarily and specifically responsible as the key teacher of the church. In some denominations he is categorically stated to be the head of the educational program; in others his position is less clear, but in nearly all churches the pastor is expected to have general charge of the educational program. He may well exercise this leadership in conjunction with the official board. He may, of course, delegate part of his responsibility to an assistant pastor or a director of Christian education. The responsibility ultimately however is the pastor's.

From the viewpoint of Christian nurture, in the fourth place, the whole church is a school. In earlier generations much of the educational work of the church was carried out through auxiliary agencies, such as the old-fashioned Sunday school, the women's auxiliary, and the youth groups (Christian Endeavor, BYPU, Epworth League, etc.). In some communities it is still the custom to carry on the educational work through agencies that are distinctly separate from the church. It has seldom been wise for the church to let its task of Christian nurture be carried on by agencies that are not responsible to the church itself, either at the denominational or at the congregational level. Exceptions such as the World's Student Christian Federation prove the rule. When educational agencies are set up outside of the official policies of the church and not under the governing boards, there is a hiatus between the educational work of the church and the rest of its life. The entire life of the church ought to be under its official board (or congregation). Agencies that grow up apart from the church tend to be divisive, creating false loyalties. They also are likely to be inadequate, for the whole church needs to be active in the whole teaching program. In some sections there arose not only folk afflicted with "Sunday schoolitis," but also folk infected with the virus of what may be called "Sunday school theology." Both heresy and moralism and whitewashed secularism are sometimes taught in such extra-church organizations. It is hard enough to have sound teaching even when it is under the auspices of the church. A teacher in a main-line church, for instance, is reputed to have said, "Jesus Christ was the greatest segregationist who ever lived." False teaching!

The church has learned, therefore, to have not a Sunday school as a separate agency, but a Sunday church school that is definitely under the official board of the church and that functions as the church teaching. Organized groups for the women, the men, and the young people are now considered a part of the church too. This difference is not trivial; it is fundamental.

Christian teaching is for all ages from cradle to grave. It is for all groups within the church. It cannot be limited to the traditional study groups. Adults desperately need to be given Christian education, to wrestle with the Bible as it speaks to men in the midst of the twentieth century. The best churches today think in terms of a total, unified program of Christian education, carried out for all ages and all groups under the supervision and guidance of the committee on Christian education. This total unified program builds upon the past, and it has incorporated the best features of the various agencies, which once served the church. This modern education occurs in the existential present, and it points to the future. It becomes real here and now—each day. But it looks beyond the present; it expects growth and change and it labors in hope.

Marjorie Reeves wrote, "A proper family life is the only basis for a true education" and "Families are the real bricks of the church." (*Growing Up in a Modern Society,* pp. 102, 121; University of London Press, London, 4th ed., 1956.) The next chapter will develop this theme that church and family work together as communities of Christian nurture.

Finally, the church needs the best possible leaders. Every Sunday over two million earnest folk give of their time and energy in Sunday church school teaching. The quality of their work runs from the pathetic to the magnificent. Some churches are far more richly blessed with natural leadership than are others. Some churches have plenty of good teaching material; others have almost none. And it is foolish to think that just anyone can teach the Christian faith. That is, formally. Every Christian does some teaching informally and unconsciously, but for conscious, formal teaching certain qualities of leadership help greatly. One simple list of qualities follows: consecrated folk who live in Christ, the most important quality of all; folk who know and love people in particular as well as in general; folk who know the Bible and Christian doctrine and ethics, who are willing to learn; folk who are "apt to teach." Less significant but in some situations needed are the qualities of attractiveness, culture, and winsomeness.

Every Christian leader is also a sinner. No pastor and no teacher is sinless. All are touched with the frailty of mortality. All are fighting a civil war within, though in some the civil war is relatively quiescent, while in others it is raging fiercely. Few if any teachers meet all the qualifications set forth in any listing. But the church has to try to select the best possible leaders who at the moment are available. Further, the church has the duty to work out a long-range leadership recruitment and training program. This particular book was the outgrowth of such a program. The church takes the best leadership it can get now, and then it tries to develop still better leadership.

Just as the two major political parties in 1960 left to one side a whole generation of able leadership to call forth a dynamic younger group of leaders, so it is that in many a church some able present leaders will be passed over as dynamic new and younger leadership is trained. Actually, no leader should be given a lifetime job in Christian education. It may inflate a man's ego to be able to say, "I was teacher of the men's Bible class for forty years." It would have been far better for the church, however, if the leadership had been shared. One of the best of the recent trends in Christian education is that of rotation. The idea is simple and is capable of variations to fit local needs. A person teaches three years, then is off a year, and then returns to a leadership function, probably to the same spot he held before, possibly to another. There are certain persons who for good reasons ought not to be rotated every three years. The principle when applied to superintendents or departmental superintendents probably ought to cover a longer period of service, say five or six years. It has been found that many able people are willing to take on a specific task for a given period but fight shy of committing themselves to a job indefinitely, i.e., "forever." Rotation shares leadership, develops additional leaders, and gives needed rest and opportunity for additional training on the part of jaded teachers. It also on occasion makes it easy to shift a round peg from a square hole.

The preceding paragraph has implied that no leader should be given a lifetime job in a particular spot in the church organization. It also implies that no leader is indispensable. Many a church has found to its amazement that when so and so rotates, the work goes on beautifully, even taking on new life because someone has come in with fresh ideas and youthful vigor to carry on the good work. No leader is indispensable, not even the minister. In fact, the wise minister is always trying to train laymen for particular phases of leadership, in evangelism, stewardship, education. A minister is indispensable but no particular minister is indispensable, and the more laymen a minister is able to enlist in fruitful and meaningful service the better. It would in fact be grand if most of the routine visitation, organizational mechanics, and administrative headaches were cared for by the laity so the minister could spend more time on the things for which he is primarily trained and which he can do better than any other. The more good laymen that are at work in meaningful tasks, not busywork, for the church, the more time the minister has for study, for sermon preparation, for prayer and meditation, for the intimate pastoral counseling and the pastoral functions which only he can carry out.

How to Teach This Lesson

It would be possible to begin this session with a lecture on the Biblical view of the church. Better still, divide into small groups, each of which is assigned a list of carefully selected Bible passages on the church. Let each group discuss the meaning of these references, and then report to the entire group its findings. Include such metaphors as body, vine, temple, bride, and people of God. Any good book on the church, such as Donald Miller's *The Nature and Mission of the Church* (John Knox Press, 1957), can serve as a useful resource. *A Theological Word Book of the Bible,* edited by Alan Richardson (The Macmillan Company, 1951), and *A Companion to the Bible,* edited by J. J. von Allmen (Oxford University Press, 1958), are invaluable for such studies.

Another approach would be to divide into buzz groups, which would consider the question, What is our church teaching by its life? and report to the whole class. A variation would be for each buzz group to consider a specific aspect of the topic.

IV

Church and Family as Partners

One of the main themes in the reformation of Christian education is that church and family must work together as partners in Christian nurture. Gone is the naïve idea that just as you send your child to public school for an education, so you send him to Sunday church school for his Christian education. The church school is not a substitute for, but a supplement to, Christian nurture in the home. The major denominational boards of Christian education now have departments of church and family. Two great denominations, the United Presbyterians in the U.S.A., and the Episcopalians, have built their church school curriculums on the philosophy that the primary responsibility for Christian nurture lies with the family and that the church must guide parents in their efforts with their children as well as supplement parental training with group study in the church school. The Presbyterian Church in the United States is building its new curriculum on similar principles. Other great denominations are bringing into their materials suggestions for parent-teacher co-operation as well as articles designed to give guidance to parents in their role as Christian educators. Church-home co-operation is one of the clearest and strongest trends in Christian education.

It was indeed unfortunate that in its modern form the Sunday church school arose outside of the church. Started by Robert Raikes in Gloucester, England, in 1780, for underprivileged boys, to teach them reading, writing, arithmetic, and religion, the Sunday school movement spread rapidly. Though it quickly became specifically a religious institution, it was not until 1910 that the Sunday school was definitely brought under the auspices of the major denominations, with the formation of the Sunday School

Council of Evangelical Denominations. As late as 1960, the writers have known of Sunday church schools that considered themselves separate institutions from the church and not only operated on separate budgets but contended that neither pastor nor official board had any business trying to "run" the Sunday school.

Had the church been wiser, it would have brought the Sunday school under its wing from the beginning. In that event, it might have remained truer to the Biblical understanding of Christian education. The Bible tells us that the church should teach the adults, and the adults then will teach the children. Deuteronomy 6:4-9 is the key passage: "Hear, O Israel: The Lord our God is one Lord; and you shall love the Lord your God with all your heart, and with all your soul, and with all your might. And these words which I command you this day shall be upon your heart; and you shall teach them diligently to your children, and shall talk of them when you sit in your house, and when you walk by the way, and when you lie down, and when you rise. And you shall bind them as a sign upon your hand, and they shall be as frontlets between your eyes. And you shall write them on the doorposts of your house and on your gates."

These words in Deuteronomy show that God's plan of religious nurture is for the parents to have engraved on their hearts the great words of faith—the great words expressive of the deep relationship to the Heavenly Father, the one Lord God to whom we owe supreme love. Being deeply related to God themselves by walk and by talk, by all the circumstances of daily life in the home, and by special religious rites and rituals, the parents teach the children the meaning of life and faith and the love of God. Adults were taught by prophet and by priest, and even by the scribes or wise men. After the Babylonian captivity was over, the synagogue appeared in Jewish communities. The synagogue had a school as an integral part, and in the school the Old Testament was at the heart of the curriculum. The synagogue was not intended to supplant the work of the parents in religious nurture.

The New Testament does not state in so many words that the Christian families, like the old Hebrew families, were expected to bear primary responsibility for Christian nurture. But indirectly the evidence is strong. For the New Testament calls the church the New Israel (I Cor. 5:7; 10:1-6; Gal. 3:14-29; Col. 2:11; I Peter 2:1-10). It also speaks of household baptisms (Acts 16:33;

18:8; I Cor. 1:16; 7:14), and although we have no proof that there were infants in these households, the probability is great that there were infants. This is one of the lines of argument favoring infant baptism. Even those churches which do not practice infant baptism are likely today to place great emphasis upon work with children and upon the Christian home.

The gist of the matter is this: Both church and family are nurturing communities. The church has the responsibility of giving Christian nurture to all its people. It is particularly responsible for giving adult members deep and broad and meaningful training in Christian nurture—in worship and in service, in study and in the total life of the congregation, and in the lengthening outreach of the church into all the world. In God's plan as revealed in the Bible, the church teaches the parents and the parents teach the children. In God's plan as revealed in the findings of modern behavioral sciences, parents inevitably and inescapably teach their children their own religious views and attitudes, and their own interpretation of the meaning and the values of life. Modern psychology, whatever the brand, teaches that the first five years of life are extremely important. In the five preschool years the child learns to talk, to communicate with others, to walk, to think, to control bowel and bladder, to identify himself as a person unique and individual, to relate to others easily or with difficulty, to be loved and so to love, to accept himself or to hate himself. And so on down the line. The first five years of life are not finally determinative of what the child is to become, but they lay down the foundations of future personality, character, and philosophy. The child is not helplessly bound by what happens in the first five years. He continues to *become,* and never does he outgrow the possibility of change, even of radical change, in philosophy or character patterns. Each passing year, however, lessens the likelihood of drastic change. Now in these first five years the child *absorbs* the religious attitudes, though not the theology, of his parents. By osmosis, as it were, he learns to trust first in a parental figure and in time in a less fallible parental figure—the God in whom his parents trust. By direct teaching, by family prayers, by family relationship to church, by the atmosphere of the family life, he learns the ABC's of the Christian faith, just as he learns the ABC's of the family's political and economic views. It is possible in later years for the child to rebel against the articulate or inarticulate views of his parents in religion or politics or economics. But such rebellion is not likely before adolescence and where the teaching and the life have been vital and sincere and clear in any of these areas, the child in mature years will probably turn back to his early training. Essentially he retains the basic philosophy or theology of his parents with modifications due to changing times and his own individuality.

Humanly speaking, the key Biblical doctrine of the covenant was built upon this elemental fact of human nature, that the child has practically an organic relationship with his parents, as Horace Bushnell put it, so that the child becomes what his parents are.

There are two nurturing communities, the church and the home. Sociologically the family is the primary community; psychologically the family is where one gains his fundamental attitudes, his basic life philosophy, and his character structure; and religiously the family is where the child gains his religious orientation and receives his initial, foundational religious experiences. The covenant of God with his people, the church, begun with Abraham and continuing to this day, is eternal witness to God's fatherly concern for his children. The laws of personality development are on the side of the Biblical view that parents bear primary responsibility for the teaching of religion to their children. The church is right in understanding itself as the secondary community that supplements and guides the work of the primary group, the family. And surely the covenant is rooted in something more dependable than in the normal dynamics of human personality. The covenant has such deep meaning not only because it is psychologically sound to believe that children tend to become what the parents are, but primarily because God has promised to be with his people and with their children. In essence God said to Abraham, I will bless you, and your seed in you, and through you I will bless all the families of the earth (Gen. 12:1-3). The church as covenant community inherits the promise and the task: being blessed, the church must herald the gospel that others may become part of the covenant community.

In terms of Reformed theology, God in his merciful condescension established a covenant with his people. God called Abraham, and gave him a covenant, and his seed after him. By virtue of the covenant, and the people of the covenant, all the nations of the earth were to be blessed (Gen. 12:1-3, 7; 17:1-14, 21; 18:18-19).

In Biblical theology it is axiomatic that the covenant of grace is one of the main keys to the Bible. The covenant of grace was made with Abraham and his seed, but it was also for the church of the New Testament and for us. A covenant is an agreement between two or more persons. The agreement made with Abraham, symbol of God's chosen people, and in a sense of all mankind, was not a mere legal or business contract. The covenant was an act of God's free grace, wherein he said in effect, "I will be your God, and you will be my people."

God expected man to obey his will and his word. God on his side gave the assurance of his eternal love for mankind, the blessed certainty that he would be faithful to his promises. The covenant meant that God had chosen for himself a people, to whom he would give himself unfailingly and with enduring love. The covenant people, so richly blessed with the deep certainty of God's unfailing love, were to be a blessing to all the world. They were called to bear witness to the world, to be a mission to the world, to be the community through which the world would come to salvation.

God did not intend to bargain with his people but graciously to give them a covenant whose mercies far exceeded what man could offer, his obedience and love. God was faithful to the covenant, but man was unfaithful. (Read again the tragic reminder of this enshrined in The Book of Hosea. See also Jesus' lament over Jerusalem [Matt. 23:37-39].) Rightly and inevitably rituals and ceremonies were set up to be reminders of the covenant. The prophets came to see that Israel could not keep the covenant faithfully. Jeremiah foretold a new covenant to be written not on tablets of stone, as at the supremely important covenant renewal at Sinai (Ex., chs. 19 and 24), but to be written upon their hearts (Jer. 31:1, 31-34). The old covenant was fulfilled; the new covenant came to be in Jesus Christ. There came a night in an upper room when our Lord, true man offering perfect obedience and perfect love to his Father in heaven, said to a tiny band of disciples, "This cup is the new covenant in my blood" (I Cor. 11:25). Thomas Torrance, in his superb introduction to the Catechisms of the Reformed Church (*The School of Faith*, Harper & Brothers, 1959), agrees with John Calvin that the sum and substance of the covenant of grace is Jesus Christ. Important as is the covenant, therefore, we finally interpret the Bible not in terms of the covenant but in terms of Jesus Christ. The covenant has been interpreted legalistically; Jesus Christ can only be interpreted dynamically and responded to in loving obedience. By virtue of our faith-union with Christ, we can now respond in love and in faithful obedience to the gracious will of our Father. "So one man's act of righteousness leads to acquittal and life for all men." (Rom. 5:18.) Thus did Paul describe the meaning of our identification with Christ.

Most Christians believe that the covenant was made with believers and their children. The covenant that God made with Abraham and his seed is also for present-day Christians and their offspring. This is the fundamental reason for infant baptism. A study of the service of infant baptism will reveal that in presenting a child for baptism, the parents (or godparents in some churches) renew their covenant vows with the Lord, and the church joins with them. In the Presbyterian service the minister says to the congregation: "This child is now received into Christ's church: and you the people of this congregation in receiving this child promise with God's help to be his sponsor to the end that he may confess Christ as his Lord and Savior and come at last to his eternal kingdom. Jesus said, Whoso shall receive one such little child in my name receiveth me" (*The Book of Common Worship,* 1946; p. 123).

It is because of the covenant of grace that the churches which believe in infant baptism treat the offspring of believing parents as members. And therefore such churches agree with Horace Bushnell's famous dictum that the child should grow up always thinking of himself as a Christian. He does not have to wait for adulthood to be dramatically converted to Christianity; he already is a Christian. Of course when he reaches the age of responsibility he must confirm the vows that his parents took; he must commit himself to Jesus Christ as his Lord and Savior. In churches that so interpret the covenant of grace, the responsibility of church and family is to create such an atmosphere of Christian worship, Christian life, and Christian love that the child will naturally and normally be led into ever-deepening realization of what it means to be a child of the covenant. Just when regeneration occurs only God knows, but that the Holy Spirit does move in the life of the child of believing parents is part of the meaning of the covenant.

No man and no church can "save" a human being; only God in his infinite power, wisdom, and love can do that. Our task in Christian education, believing in the covenant, is to prepare the conditions, to create a wholesome atmosphere, to so live that the child seeing us will see Christ in us. . . . The time comes when he affirms for himself the covenant into which he was born.

Rooted and grounded in the promises of God, the family becomes the primary teacher of religion. Yet the New Testament warns us that the family is never an end in itself, that indeed it may take on the form of an idol (Matt. 10:37-38; Mark 3:34-35; 10:28-30; Luke 11:27-28; 14:26). The family continually needs to be taught by the larger family of God, which is the church. God's Holy Spirit, speaking to his church in and through his Word, speaks also to the families that constitute the church. The church through the centuries has received wonderful guidance and has a store of wisdom to transmit to its member families. And the church has its present life and mission as well as its past glorious heritage to share with its members. No family should try to teach the Christian faith solely "on its own," without reference to the fund of experience and wisdom of the church. Through a score of ways, the church teaches the adults who in turn teach their children.

Adult education should be the most significant aspect of modern Christian education, but in many places it is still the weakest. The church teaches its adults through the corporate worship services perhaps more powerfully than in any other way. Teaching sermons, and at times inspirational sermons, in the context of common worship, probably do more to inform and inspire and challenge adults than any other approach. Preaching, however, is not enough. Adults need to meet together in groups to *discuss* the Christian faith and its meaning for life today. Some pastors are courageous enough to let a group of adults raise questions and discuss their sermons. Some who have done so have humbly learned how difficult is the art of communication, and have become better ministers as a result. Adults learn best when they are given opportunity to raise questions, to air their own views, to struggle with new ideas, to evaluate frankly old ideas about which they have always had reservations. In short, adults learn best by *thinking*. So do youth.

The church, therefore, is now working diligently to strengthen its program of adult education. There is less emphasis on age group distinctions, more emphasis on interest groups. There may be valid place for age group distinctions from time to time (men over fifty do better at dart ball than at baseball), but interests are of vast importance. Adults of all ages are interested in some elemental questions such as: Who is Jesus Christ? Why suffering? Should being a Christian make any difference in one's racial attitudes? Is there a Christian philosophy of marriage? What is the church? Adults of all ages are interested in and need to know much about the sweep of the Bible story, the vast panorama of the unfolding self-revelation of God in his mighty acts toward his chosen people. Adults of all ages need to learn for themselves the lessons the church has learned from its own history, so full of tragic blunders and glorious victories, so full of heresy or folly and of theological wisdom and human goodness. Adults of all ages need to learn what it means to be truly loyal to Jesus Christ in all of life's relationships, what, in short, it means to live the Christian life in one's vocation, in one's home, in one's social order, in one's world—under the shadow of the H-bomb, as well as under "the shadow of a great rock in a weary land" (Isa. 32:2, KJV).

Adults need to know, and the church must teach them. When the adults have become soundly Christian in doctrine and in life, they will do an infinitely better job of nurturing their own children in the Christian faith and life. Sunday church school is not just for children and young people, it is also for adults! Manifestly, adults need to learn in many other ways and places than in Sunday church school, so there are various adult study groups, prayer cells, organizations by age or by sex or by special interest. The main thing is, adults must learn more and more about the Christian faith and life. Each church has its own program of adult education, and each congregation must adapt denominational programs and evolve its own particular programs that the adults may be taught. One word: too many organizations may spoil the soup! But experimentation is greatly needed.

How to Teach This Lesson

1. A careful study of methods of co-operation of home and church suggested in your curriculum should be made by the leader, perhaps through special assignments to individual class

members for reports. Perhaps short reports on this topic for each of the age groups would be practical.

2. Samples of the curriculum materials marked to show where parent-teacher helps are indicated, should be available so the class can scan them during the reports or discussion.

3. Your denomination's department of church and family probably has a basic pamphlet on the subject of this lesson. By all means secure it and use it.

4. A discussion could be held, particularly if you want to have two or more sessions in this area, on such topics as:

    a. How can we have a really good adult program? Try a brain-storming session on this, wherein members are free to give their wildest dreams on the subject.

    b. How can the church help the families specifically with reference to family worship?

    c. Debate: All adults should be compelled to go through a church membership class before being received as members of this particular church.

    d. Panel: Ways in which parents can help the church's program of Christian education, and ways in which the church can help the parents with Christian education in the homes.

    e. Discussion: Should we have regular family-type church suppers?

    f. What is the meaning of the baptismal vows to the family? to the church? How does your church enable parents to understand and fulfill their vows? Does your congregation carry out its baptismal promises?

    g. What are the marks of a Christian family?

5. Does your church demand so much of the time of its members that it tends to break down family life?

6. Can love of family become idolatrous? How?

V

The Place of the Bible in Christian Education

The Bible is at the heart of any curriculum in any church, for the Bible is central in the life of the church. The purpose of Christian education is not primarily to teach the Bible, but the Bible is absolutely fundamental in the curriculum because it is fundamental to the well-being of the church. No longer do we call the church school the Bible school, for today we use various materials in addition to the Bible, and we know the emphasis on the persons we teach is as important as is the emphasis on the book we teach. For years the basic idea of the Sunday church school was to teach the Bible. Still central, as far as materials are concerned, the Bible is now recognized to be not an end in itself, but a book that testifies concerning the One who is ultimately central.

Those who teach the Bible should come to an intelligent understanding of its nature. We should have some understanding of the judgment of the church's scholars concerning the nature of the inspiration of the Bible, of the fact that it does have a revelatory character, and of the fact that through the Bible God continues to speak to his church.

The Bible is a revelation of God to man, a revelation of God's nature, of his will, and of his purpose for human beings. A revelation is a self-revealing, an unfolding of one's nature, a taking away of the veil in order that one may see. God has spoken; we have a revelation. Through this revelation we are enabled to understand who God is, who Christ is, who we are. Not only does this revelation tell us of God's will, it also tells us how we can become what God intends for us to be. The Bible is significant in Christian education because it contains the records of God's mighty deeds and words, set forth in the history of God's dealings with Israel, and supremely portrayed in Jesus Christ. The mighty acts of God were for the revelation of himself to his people—then and now. When we read the Bible, we read the story of salvation. The Germans have a word for it, *Heilsgeschichte,* salvation history. The Bible contains, therefore, God's word to man, his marching orders to his church, set forth in the form of mighty deeds. The Bible has been given to us that we may know God and self and our need of salvation, as well as the Christian way of life. God has spoken; this is the fact of revelation. The Bible contains the records of God's dealings with his people in history; this is the report of the revelation (see Sherrill's *The Gift of Power,* Ch. IV). The mighty deeds of the history of salvation have been reported in words. The words of the Bible are the report of an encounter or rather a series of encounters between God and men, as God has moved mightily for the salvation of men. God has spoken, in word and in deed, and fully and finally in the Word made flesh, Jesus Christ our Lord. In the whole story of the Bible, which is the story of salvation, God has spoken to reveal himself. He has shown us that his nature is holy, sovereign love, or, if you prefer, loving, sovereign holiness. All three words are essential, whatever their order. God is Creator, Redeemer, and Guide; Father, Son, and Holy Spirit—one God. This God in his love toward us has moved in his Son that we might have life eternal. God has spoken, and we know who he is and what he is like, for we have seen his self-revelation in his Son. The revelation is in the mighty deeds; the record of it is in the Bible.

The Bible is a divine-human book. It comes to us as a divine revelation mediated through human authors. One of our professors, a stalwart conservative Old Testament scholar, and later a Moderator of the General Assembly, used to say, "The Bible has on it human fingerprints." A British writer recently made the point that all the way through we have the treasure of God in earthen vessels. "It is part of the condescension of God that he should have stooped to declare his Word through the words of fallible men. This is the pattern of divine condescension which runs through the whole of God's self-communication to man—in his incarnation in the man Jesus, in his body the church, in his use of the frail elements of water, bread, and wine in the two sacraments of the gospel. . . . All the way through, we have to discern the treasure in the earthen vessels: the divinity in Christ's humanity; his body and blood in the bread and wine; the Israel of God in that body of fallible and sinful men and women we call the church; the Word of God in the fallible words of men." (R. H. Fuller, in *Bulletin* No. 110; The SCM Book Club, Jan., 1956.)

In the Bible we have a book written by human beings, yet inspired by the Holy Spirit. The writers remained human beings; they did not become automatons. They left the imprint of their personalities upon what they wrote. This is obvious when you read the four Gospels. Each of them is different, having its own style, its own point of view. Each of them emphasizes some things and omits other things. This is exactly what we would expect if human beings led of the Spirit did the writing. Clearly, the Spirit gave them freedom to be themselves and to see the divine truth from the perspective of their own day and age. The Bible is indeed God's word to man, God's word contained in human words, and we have to see beneath the surface to see what God is saying to us. Just reading the Bible does not automatically give us God's word. We must read the Bible in the spirit of prayer and under the guidance of the Holy Spirit in the context of the understanding and interpretation the church has reached. When we read the Bible from this point of view, *and as men of faith,* we can hear God speaking to us through his book.

The fact of revelation is accepted by faith. Men have differed for centuries as to the exact manner of his revelation, the precise meaning of the inspiration of the Bible. But that God has spoken, and supremely in his Son, this surely we must all believe. God has spoken, and we know it.

The church school teacher should recognize that one ancient cliché concerning the Bible is false. "If one word of the Bible is wrong, then we can't trust any of it." Some good people have believed this, but it just is not true. The truth is, the Bible is God's word and we can trust it even if we do find inconsistencies or seeming contradictions here and there. There is no need to fear that something in the Bible may be proved to be untrue. While it is not correct to say that archaeology today is steadily proving the Bible to be true, it is correct to say that the researches of the archaeologists on the whole are testifying to the essential accuracy of the Holy Scriptures. We do not have to prove the Bible, rather, we take it on faith. It may be possible to show that this particular event happened just as recorded, but it is totally impossible to prove that the God portrayed in the Bible actually exists. The way of life portrayed in the Bible cannot be proved, it has to be lived in faith. "Wherefore by their fruits ye shall know them." (Matt. 7:20, KJV.) In the end the Bible is a book that speaks to men of faith and only men of faith can understand it.

Anybody can understand the facts. The history of the Bible can be taught to anybody, but the Bible is God's story. We can believe in God only by faith, and we can understand the Bible only by faith. This book teaches us of the God-man, and this story is either a fairy tale or the deepest truth in the world. A man does not believe in Jesus Christ until God moves in his heart. If we want to believe, we are already men of faith. "I believe; help my unbelief!" (Mark 9:24.) When we can say this, we are moving toward faith. Faith is our believing response to the word of God. We know in our heart whether we have it or not. We may recognize that our faith is imperfect; most of us have an imperfect faith. There may be times when we have doubts; every Christian has doubts. But if our foundational attitude is that of faith; and if we read the Word in prayer, we will hear God speaking to us.

The Christian faith is the belief that the church has reached through the centuries as the result of its long and careful study of the Bible. The faith is something that can in a sense be enshrined in a creed or confession. Yet in another sense the faith is dynamic, existential, contextual, the active beliefs of the pilgrim people on their march to the Promised Land.

The Bible is not all on one level. There are two testaments. While both testaments contain and convey the word of God, so that a genuine unity is undeniable, yet it is also true that the Christian must always interpret the Old Testament in the light of the fuller revelation of God in the New Testament.

Nobody really believes that all parts of the Bible are of equal value. The Bible of Everyman has some pages far more smudged with use than are other pages. All of us would in fact admit at once that we prefer to feed our souls on certain passages and perhaps rather shamefully neglect other passages. No part of the Bible is valueless, but some passages contain little more than information, whereas other passages cry to be lovingly memorized and lived by. John Calvin wrote a commentary on practically every book of the Bible, but he did not write one on the book of The Revelation. The basic significance of that book is clear, but its detailed meanings probably will remain forever obscure. Ephesians or Romans or Philippians or The Acts or John or Mark, however, are astonishingly alive and meaningful, to mention a few of the more vital books of the New Testament. Space fails to tell of Luke and of Matthew, of Corinthians and of Hebrews. . . .

Both the Old Testament and the New Testament contain and convey the Word of God. A genuine unity between the two testaments is now generally recognized. Some groups still tend to say, "We are a New Testament church." There are denominations that in effect write off the Old Testament. Their scholars read it, but their constant refrain is, "The New Testament says . . ." Some stalwart Christian scholars who teach Old Testament strongly disagree with this approach. Although we recognize that a fundamental unity exists between the Old Testament and the New Testament, we must remember a basic fact. The Christian does not start with the Old Testament and then move to the New Testament. In the historical sense, of course, he does just this, but in another sense he has to read the Old Testament with the spectacles of the New Testament on his eyes. If he takes the Old Testament without the New Testament, he finds material that simply cannot be reconciled with the Christian faith. There are passages in the Old Testament that apparently portray a God of wrath and vengeance. When he gets to Hosea and Isaiah, he sees the mercy of God set forth beautifully. If he reads certain passages in The Book of Judges, for instance, without any knowledge of the later prophets, or the Gospels, he finds a God whom it would be hard to worship. He finds in the Bible in various places folk whose actions he would not want his children to copy. When the Old Testament is understood in the light of its environment, and with a knowledge of its more glorious portions such as the Second Isaiah (chs. 40 to 66), and in the light of the New Testament, one can find a place for its more difficult passages. The Christian must look at the Old Testament in the light of the New Testament, and must recognize that some of these very difficult passages of the Old Testament do not fully describe the nature of the God and Father of our Lord Jesus Christ. The human fingerprints show through here and there. Although almost without exception the Old Testament is in advance of the ethical standards of its day, the Christian takes his stand in the New Testament. If we do not look at the

Old Testament through the eyes of the New Testament, then we might as well write off the Christian faith and consider ourselves still Jews.

On the other hand, granted all of this, we cannot understand the New Testament without understanding the Old. This is a paradox, because there is some material in the Old Testament that we have to recognize is on a sub-Christian level. The Old Testament does, however, contain the foundations for that which came to be in the New Testament. In it are the promises of the Coming One who in the reign of Caesar Augustus became incarnate. In it are the great basic facts of God as creator and as sovereign and as a God who is concerned with persons. In it are the revelations of the mighty deeds of God with his chosen people. In it are the Ten Commandments, matchless summary of the Law. In it are devotional psalms unsurpassed in beauty and worth. In it is the one great story of the God who chooses for himself a people and makes a covenant with them, a God indeed who saves his people and then sends them out to bring the world to himself. A fine Christian psychiatrist, a very able man, once commented that he did not see why the Sunday school lesson he had to teach next Sunday was on the exodus from Egypt. Why, he wondered, isn't our lesson on something current and relevant. Little did he realize that to Biblical scholars there is no more important story in the Old Testament than the story of the exodus from Egypt. Through his servant Moses, God redeemed the people of Israel from their bondage. This is a parallel to the way in which God later saved mankind through his Son. Through his Son Jesus Christ, God has set the human race free from its bondage of sin. One does not understand the New Testament unless he is familiar with these Old Testament facts and mighty deeds. To be a good and informed Christian, one should know something of the salvation history, of the way in which God made the covenant with Abraham and with his descendants after him, and of the way in which the people of the Old Testament turned away from this God again and again, and finally of the way in which there was not a whole people but only a small remnant of faithful people saved. Some able Biblical scholars say this remnant finally was reduced to one man and that man was God. Then he started again the building of the church. This is the beautiful story of the people of God, the *Heilsgeschichte*.

We understand the Old Testament through the eyes of the New. We cannot understand the New Testament unless we understand the Old. In both testaments the Bible does genuinely contain and convey a divine revelation, which is consummated in Jesus Christ. "In many and various ways God spoke of old to our fathers by the prophets; but in these last days he has spoken to us by a Son." (Heb. 1:1-2.)

It is our task as teachers of the word to understand the nature of the Bible, to have an appreciation of its message, and to make a response in faith to the Word of God contained in Holy Scripture. When we have met Jesus Christ face to face in the Bible, then we can begin to help others to meet him face to face. It is our task as teachers to help people to know the Bible, to understand its story, to have a grasp of its panorama, to have a deep understanding of the Biblical perspective on life, and to realize that the way the Bible looks at things often is different from our modern secularized perspectives. It is our primary task to help people to meet in the words of the Bible the living word of God in Jesus Christ. In the written words we read the word that is life itself. He both portrays the meaning of life and gives meaning to life. The Bible is our primary document in Christian education, our key textbook, the source of the power and life of the whole Christian education program. We go to Sunday church school not only to learn the facts of the Bible, important though they be; we also go to Sunday church school in order to come face to face with Jesus Christ. We have many lesser purposes as we teach the Bible, but our supreme purpose is to deepen the relationships that inhere in the divine-human encounter. We teach this book that people may meet God face to face, may gain the Biblical point of view upon life, and may begin to live in our modern world as people under the influence of the word of God.

The Bible is not an end in itself. It is not to be worshiped as the fourth person of the Godhead. It is an ageless witness to Jesus Christ and a mighty instrument for the preaching and teaching of the way and will and word of God for man. Though we do not worship the Bible, we well may cherish it deeply and read it faithfully and absorb its language, so that the Biblical vocabulary becomes the language of our souls.

In recent years, perhaps, we have taken the Bible with lip service too seriously but really have not taken it seriously with our lives.

We should teach the Bible facts and the Bible story, not as ends in themselves but as an aid to our ultimate purpose of bringing people face to face with the Lord. By the time they have finished high school, our young people for instance should have a clear grasp of the sweep of the Bible story, they should know that it contains and conveys the Word of God to man. They will know that some things are recounted in the Old Testament, some in the New. They will gain some sense of the history of events; they will know the primary truths and the grand story of salvation. They should face the great questions of life in the light of the Bible and be taught something of the meaning of life, the answer of the Bible to life's significant questions: Who am I? Why am I here? Where am I going? Who is God? Why did Jesus Christ come? And who is he, anyhow? What does it mean to be saved? What does it mean to live in Christ? What is it to be a citizen of two worlds? What is the Christian view of sex? What is it to be called of God? The light the Bible casts on these great questions should be known by adults as well as by youth, of course. It is good for youth to know the specific stories of the Bible, but it is also important for youth to know the fundamental Biblical perspective on life and the "old, old story." There are, of course, specific passages that youth ought to know intimately; everyone has his own list. Our list would surely include the first three chapters of Genesis, the Sermon on the Mount, the Passion Week narrative, Luke, chs. 2 and 15, and a host of other great passages. Youth needs to know that as we read the Bible thoughtfully and prayerfully in the light of all the help we can receive from other Christians, and in prayer for the guidance of the Holy Spirit, we can hear the word of God. Youth needs to know the Christ who is set forth in the Scriptures, not simply as a good man of the long ago but as the living Lord and Savior of us all. Youth needs to wrestle with the dynamic principles of living set forth in the Scriptures without becoming prey to legalism or moralism.

Now young people do not get all of this in the kindergarten department. They begin at home and then continue in the childrens' division to get attitudes and atmosphere, and by the time they are in the junior department, they ought to be able to grasp the Biblical panorama. At the end of the junior high department they ought to have a firmer grasp of the sweep of the story and an understanding of the basic Biblical perspectives.

Until the Holy Spirit opens up its meaning for us, the Bible is just another book, albeit a good one. This is not heresy; it is sound orthodoxy, found in John Calvin, in the Westminster Confession of Faith, and in many great Christian thinkers. To many people the Bible is simply good or even great literature; only to people of faith is the Bible the word of God. When the Holy Spirit opens up its meaning for us, and not until then, it becomes to us the word of God. "The inner testimony of the Spirit" in our hearts is, then, all-important, for only through his work in us do we hear God himself speak in his Book.

The Christian educator should live with his Bible. The best Sunday church school teachers know the Bible intimately. This does not mean that they have to know the minute details of the Bible. It does mean that they should understand the spirit of the Bible, know what it says, and make its words and its vocabulary a part of their lives. Few teachers start off with an intimate knowledge of the Bible; they grow into this. No young minister goes out to his first pastorate with a full knowledge of the Bible, nor does he know it backward and forward. This kind of knowledge is the work of a lifetime, and the Sunday school teacher is not unlike the minister in this regard. He starts out with what he has and keeps going. Living with the Bible, he begins in time to embody its spirit in his life. In his daily life he becomes a living epistle. (Lest you be frightened, Paul first used this phrase in writing to the far-from-perfect group of Christians in the church at Corinth.)

Some Practical Implications

The Bible is our primary curriculum tool. In its own right it constantly bears witness to the eternal Word. And the church has long since learned that it must keep close to the Bible if it is to keep close to its Lord. In its work of teaching, the church makes full use of the Bible as the means of educating its members in the Christian faith. The Bible, however, is an adult book written by adults for adults. Adults should engage in Bible study faithfully and regularly. The family whose Bible study is limited to that done by ten-year-old Susie and six-year-old Timmie is a family sorely lacking in Biblical understanding. If we are to take seriously the concept that Christian education is primarily for adults who in turn will teach their children, then somehow we shall have to find ways of engaging adults in serious Bible study. For most adults this can best be done on Sunday morning; it does need to be done sometime, someplace, with regularity and with increasing depth. Experimentation is needed to find more effective ways of engaging adults in genuine Bible study. Not all adults are at present interested in such study, but those who realize the plight of man and the profound Christian answer to man's need, are ready to begin to do real Bible study. Their name is not yet legion, but the tribe is rapidly increasing.

The Bible is an adult book; therefore, when used with those who are not adults, there should be careful gradation. The church school has long accepted the need of gradation. We know that some sections of the Bible are totally beyond the comprehension of children. When without gradation we teach all parts of the Bible to all ages, we misuse the Bible. Intended for adults, its message should, as it were, be strained through the sieve of adult faith before being taught to children. The book of Romans, for instance, which is admitted to be one of the pivotal books of the Bible, is difficult for the average adult to understand, and is completely beyond the comprehension of children below the junior years. Genesis, which is also a great key book, contains passages that are seldom read in corporate worship, passages that are never studied in the church school. Genesis contains stories of incest, adultery, harlotry, homosexuality, and crude murder. These stories are factual, realistic, and clearly for adults. Some parents in the intimacy of their own home may be willing to read and discuss these passages with their children, but most parents probably would not be at ease in doing so. The Biblical view of sex is that it is good, a gift of God, to be richly enjoyed as a way of expressing true henosis (one-flesh) love of mate for mate. This Biblical view desperately needs to be taught to our youth, but several of the Genesis stories are of the misuse of sex, not of its proper use.

Current church school literature is increasingly careful as to what should be used with children. Sometimes curriculum editors are overly cautious, and sometimes they underestimate what children in our generation are capable of taking in stride, but they are correct in being careful in selecting passages for children. It is impossible to mark off the Bible in sections appropriate for each age group, for the Bible was not written for various age groups. Further, many passages that are clearly for adults contain overtones that can be grasped by children who are much too young to understand the concept but who can feel the emotions and the mood of the passage. The Twenty-third Psalm is such a passage. Some three-year-olds can sense its deep and moving tones, yet not even the seventy-year-old can fully understand all of its profundities. The parables of Jesus are not easily grasped by little children who tend to be literalistic.

The point at issue is clear: the Bible is so adult that when taught to children, carefully graded selections have to be made. It is entirely proper to tell little children some of the lovely stories in words they can understand rather than in the words of the Bible. It is right to put great Bible truths in simple language for children, but it is never right to water down the Bible in order to teach it to children. For instance, some Easter lessons have left out all reference to the death and resurrection of Jesus and have talked about the new life in nature. Adults are tempted to sugarcoat the demands of the gospel for unselfish living, for surrender, and for following the example of Jesus; it would be foolish to deliberately train children to sugar-coat the Bible.

Church school teachers should realize that the graded selections from the Bible that appear in the printed curricular materials have been chosen with utmost care by experts who have studied the psychological findings concerning the ability of each age to work with concepts. If the editor has underestimated the ability of one local group, he has overestimated the ability of another such group. Each teacher therefore needs to know his own class so well that he knows when to step up and when to step down the language of the printed materials.

At the risk of seeming to be repetitious, let us remember that our main aim in Christian education is not only to teach the facts or even the stories of the Bible, but to use facts and stories and teachings in order to help people to have a meeting with the God of the Bible. In line with the principle of gradation, we teach facts and stories when the children are supposedly mature enough to grasp them. What is fundamental in the teaching of little children is that they accept the spirit of the Bible. Every four-year-old has experienced sin, fall, repentance, forgiveness, and grace. Humanly speaking, he has gone through the story of salvation in his living in his family. He has learned something of the grace of God through the grace shown to him by his parents. He has learned something of the power and love of God through the power and love of his parents. He has also learned something of the fact of order, of discipline, of judgment, that he has to live within a given framework. By the age of two and one half the average child is ready to rebel against the framework of his environment (his parents and their rules). By three and one half he has learned to live within the limits. If the rebellion does not crop up again at five, it will at twelve or thirteen. If the parents are Christian, the child, in the context of his struggle to find himself and become an independent person without becoming an obnoxiously selfish person, learns through the experiences of living in the Christian family much of the nature of the gospel. To a degree, this same ability to absorb atmosphere and spirit and to intuit meaning is also predominant in the teaching-learning process of the early years in the church school.

Children need to go to church with their parents from time to time. In many communities children can and should start going to church with their parents by the time they start going to school. Of course they cannot understand much of the sermon, though they may surprise you with how much they do take in of the preacher's meaning and attitude. The church worship service that is sufficiently liturgical to have certain responses, prayer, and congregational participation can be genuinely meaningful to children. On the other hand, the sermon-centered service is likely to be boring to most children. Let them repeat the Apostles' Creed (whose sonorous phrases impart some meaning at the emotional level, the level by which we live), let there be occasional unison reading of Ps. 100 and Ps. 23, let there be the Lord's Prayer, let there be the singing of the great hymns of the church; and the child who has been trained in church school to participate in corporate worship will find it a meaningful experience. Some churches find the children's sermon helpful, but it is easy for children's sermons to become moralistic and mediocre. The child will profit more from good solid exposition of Scripture, illuminated by a gracious spirit and apt illustrations.

In the church school, the Bible ought to be present and used. By the junior age, children should have their own Bibles, and they should be taught how to use them, how to find their way around in the Bible. The session or official board probably will wish to make the decision as to which translation of the Bible is to be used throughout the Sunday church school. For years the King James Version was the accepted Bible; now more and more church schools are using the Revised Standard Version, which has the advantage of being both more scholarly and in language more nearly like that spoken today, yet has retained much of the magnificent literary flavor of the King James Version.

We believe it is still good to memorize Scripture. Children's experts tend to suggest that memorization be limited to the verses that are directly related to particular lessons. We believe that while this procedure is good, it is inadequate. There ought to be an effort to have pupils memorize some of the great Scripture passages. A few of the psalms should be known by every child before he is ready for school, and also a few verses from the New Testament. Later the child can learn the Christmas story; I Cor., ch. 13; Rom., ch. 12; the Beatitudes, and other great passages. He also should memorize the Apostles' Creed and if he is in a liturgical church, some of the great prayers and responses. Such memorization, incidentally, should be sparked by the church school teacher but carried out at home, not during the church school hour. By the junior department, some of these materials can be used in departmental worship. And they should be used fairly often in the corporate worship of the congregation. The good teacher, of course, will endeavor to explain the background and basic meaning of the passage to be memorized. It is silly to insist that a child be able to understand everything he memorizes. He can memorize Ps. 23 or John 3:16 and have some preconceptual understanding of meaning long years before he can have a clear grasp of concept. What adult fully understands John 3:16?

If the Bible is at the heart of the curriculum, then it is not enough for the teacher to talk about what the Bible says. The class should wrestle with the passage or the material, guided by the teacher, but animatedly entering into the discussion. This means the teacher has to be willing to have his own ideas and interpretations questioned or even strongly rejected. It means that the teacher has to reach the point where he can admit that he does not know. Children from junior age up should not only have Bibles, they should take them to church on Sunday and should be encouraged to use them.

How to Teach This Lesson

This lesson can easily be lengthened into half a dozen. But the essence of an informed, intelligent, believing approach to the Bible can be dug into in one session. This is a good session for the pastor to teach, particularly if the emphasis is to fall on the nature of the Bible. If the emphasis of the lesson is to be made on the use of the Bible with children, perhaps a skilled teacher of children could lead the discussion.

If the emphasis is to fall on the use of the Bible with different age groups, perhaps members of the class could be assigned to bring in reports from reading and from interviews with able teachers.

Genesis, chs. 1 to 3, makes an excellent background from which to delve fairly deeply into ways of using the Bible with modern folk.

VI

The Persons We Teach

To whom and with whom do we communicate the gospel? Who is this creature, man? What are human beings? Is there such a thing as human nature? Such questions dig down to one of the foundations of Christian education, for our approach to our teaching task is largely determined by our view of human beings. When our second child was in the sixth grade, she came home to tell us at dinner of the argument which had waxed hot and furious at school. "Our teacher said that if a tree falls in the forest, and there is no human being nearby to hear the thud, there has been no sound. Sound depends upon hearing. If the sound waves are not heard by a human ear, then there are no sounds." An old argument, that! Words uttered to deaf ears do not make a sound! If man lives as an animal, obviously and undeniably a part of nature, but without any sense of being more than that, without any realization of obligation to the Creator, then that man cannot receive a communication about Jesus Christ. But if man is more than an animal, if there is in man something of the image of God (Gen. 1:27), if man's true nature has been manifested in Jesus Christ, so that we are to have his mind in us (Phil. 2:5-11), then man is capable of being communicated with, of receiving some sure word of God. Christian education is to be carried out on the basis of a Christian view of man.

Some Elemental Facts from Science

Christian education can and must accept the basic findings of science concerning this being we call man. All truth is of God, and if science clearly reaches a given conclusion that such and

such is a fact about man, the Christian simply accepts that fact.
He does not always accept the interpretation of the fact as given
by the scientist who begins to philosophize upon the meaning
of the fact, but he does have to accept the fact, in the provisional
sense in which science accepts facts. The theologian's interpretation of the meaning of a fact discovered by science may be far
wiser and truer than the interpretation placed upon it by the
scientist.

Beyond reasonable doubt, science has shown that man has been
on this earth a long time, not just a few thousand years, and during this vast period of time there has been a process of development. This fact surely suggests patience as we think of human
potentialities of growth either in the individual or in society.

Again, science has shown that man is an animal, one of the
mammals. Man has the same general bodily structure as the apes.
He has the same elemental life urges that surge through the blood
of monkeys, dogs, and horses. Hunger, reproduction, self-preserva-
tion—these elemental urges are real determinants of human nature. Now if man does have an inheritance of animal nature, a
genuine kinship with the brutes, then the lusts of the body will
need ever to be kept under control. Freud's id and Jung's shadow
help to remind us of this animal inheritance of man.

Man is a part of creation, with a kinship to the animals, and he
has been here a long, long time, slowly developing. These basic
facts from the realm of science, Christian education can assume.
But if we stop there, we stop with naturalism or at best humanism.

Although Christian education will accept the findings of science
—at least provisionally—it is not limited to the findings of science
in its understanding of human nature. Christian education unashamedly accepts the facts of Biblical revelation as well as the discoveries of science. The Christian believes that the approach to
truth via the scientific method is only one valid approach to truth;
another equally valid approach to truth is through divine revelation and faith responding to that revelation.

The Biblical View of Man

1. The Biblical revelation teaches that *man is a creature of God*.
"It is he that hath made us, and not we ourselves; We are his
people, and the sheep of his pasture." (Ps. 100:3, KJV.) We were

created by God, and in the very depths of our beings we are dependent upon God. We are neither self-creating nor self-sustaining. Man the creature is always dependent upon the creator. Even the supremely great gift of freedom that God has granted to us does not make us independent of God. Always the finite creature stands in need of the infinite God. The child is dependent upon the Heavenly Father. Even though God has given man dominion over the creatures (Gen. 1:28), man is not the creator but a creature.

2. Revelation teaches that *man is made in the image of God* (Gen. 1:27). This *imago Dei* is not easy to define. Many scholars take it to mean that man has the power to reason. Other scholars find the image in man's ability to have communion with God. Emil Brunner somewhere speaks of it as "man's capacity to hear (or not to hear) the word of God." Walther Eichrodt, in his brilliant little book, *Man in the Old Testament* (tr. by K. and R. Gregor Smith; SCM Press, Ltd., London, 1951), does not define the *imago Dei*, but he is in agreement with Brunner. Man, Eichrodt says, is a being whose responsibility is to obey unconditionally the will of God. Only as we are called of God and respond to his call do we reach the fullness of our humanity. Reinhold Niebuhr in philosophical language suggests that the image of God in man is man's capacity to transcend nature, and even himself. This power of self-transcendence, this ability to stand off and look at oneself, means that man is not merely an animal. Man's spirit is so made that it is capable of communing with the Eternal Spirit and is not satisfied until it does so commune. God is the Father of our spirits, and we can offer to him an even deeper love than a child can offer to its parents. And we must offer our Heavenly Father a perfect obedience.

3. But *man is a sinner*, so he does not and cannot offer God that perfect love and perfect obedience which it is his place to offer. Genesis, ch. 1, tells us that man was created in the image of God, and Gen., ch. 3, tells us that the image was marred. Man in his rebellious pride became a sinner. The *imago Dei* within us was badly marred but not hopelessly, for we are still capable of being healed and conscious of our need of healing. Sin is both the cause and the result of the marring of the image. The story of the Fall is the eternal symbol of the marred image, of the badly scratched mirror, of the essential nature of sin. Adam is every man. Man's

whole personality is shot through and through with sinfulness. That is why it is so difficult to teach the Christian faith. Man is "dead in sin." He cannot save himself. Only by grace can man be saved.

The darling angel who is so sweet and precious at six months has become at twenty-six months the little imp whose pet word is no! One night at the Louisville Southern Baptist Seminary a panel discussion was held on the topic of "Guilt." On the panel were two outstanding Christian psychiatrists, a Baptist professor of theology, and a Baptist professor of pastoral counseling. I was graciously drawn into the discussion. A Presbyterian psychiatrist, in the midst of a discussion of Freud's concept of guilt, turned to me and said, "Isn't it true that Freud is very much like Calvin in his concept of human depravity?" I answered, "Yes," for modern depth psychology, following Freud, has certainly strengthened the hands of those who believe that human depravity and original sin are not outmoded dogmas. "The heart is deceitful above all things, and desperately corrupt; who can understand it?" (Jer. 17:9.) But the Baptist professor of theology insisted that while it is true that Calvin, like Freud, teaches the depravity of human nature, Calvin, unlike Freud, also teaches that human nature is redeemable. Freud, therefore, is pessimistic, but Calvin is deeply hopeful.

4. And of course the theologian was correct! For the fourth fact that Revelation teaches about man is that *man is redeemable*. This is the gospel: God redeems man, makes of him a new creation, gives him salvation in and through Jesus Christ. This human nature that is shot through and through with sinfulness, is yet a human nature which by the grace of God can be made new. Human nature can be changed!

5. In the fifth place, even though man is redeemable, as long as he lives on earth *he is not capable of reaching perfection* of character. That is what Rom., ch. 7, teaches. Man so long as he lives bears within him a conflict, not between flesh and spirit in the usual Greek sense of body as evil and soul as good, but rather the conflict is between that which is worldly and that which is truly spiritual within us. More sharply, the conflict is between our will to good and our proneness to evil. So with Paul we human beings say again and again: "The good that I would, I do not: but the

evil which I would not, that I do" (ch. 7:19, KJV). Even redeemed man bears within himself a remnant of the old man of sin, a downward drag.

6. Revelation, in the sixth place, teaches us that *in Jesus Christ we see ourselves as we ought to be.* He is perfect man, our supreme example. He is far more, but he is that. He is the way, the truth, and the life, and the goal of our living ought to be to have the mind of Christ. As the Second Adam, he gave to the Father the perfect obedience and absolute love which the first Adam was unable to give, and in him "shall all be made alive" (I Cor. 15:22; see also Rom. 5:12-21). He who is the image of the invisible God (Col. 1:15) is true Man, and in him we know what God intends for us to be. In him our manhood comes alive.

7. Even in this world *we may have the Spirit of Christ within us.* "I live; yet not I, but Christ liveth in me," shouted Paul triumphantly. And for his converts at Colossae he prayed that each might have "Christ in you, the hope of glory." The very center of our lives is the love of Christ, the will of Christ. We strive to love what he loves and to will what he wills. We are able for all things through him who empowers us.

The Biblical view of man hinted at in these seven points contains and includes all of these points, yet is not exhausted by them, nor is it to be identified with just one or two of them. We can't understand man simply by thinking he is a sinner, or by thinking of the *imago Dei.*

The Biblical perspective is always to be held in tension with the discoveries of science. We accept both the revelation in the Bible and the revelation in nature as true, but there will always be unresolvable tensions between the two, for we are men and not God. Science, for instance, teaches correctly that man is part of nature and an animal; Christianity teaches that man is *imago Dei.* "Yet thou hast made him little less than God." (Ps. 8:5.) These facts are not really contradictory. Man *is* an animal, but far more, for he is also a son of God, which means that while man was created on the sixth day with the other animals, he was created that he might have dominion over the creatures and fellowship with the Creator. The animal inheritance of man helps to make him what he is, but his spiritual inheritance is of greater importance still.

Some Implications for the Christian Educator

If man be a child of God, then each human being ought to be treated with genuine respect. All men are God's children and all men are to be treated with respect and dignity, as ends and not as means. This principle covers such matters as age and sex and class and color and nationality. Even more deeply, if persons are creations of the Creator, then we must love them all. "Thou shalt love thy neighbor as thyself." That unselfish, self-giving love depicted in I Cor., ch. 13, which Bible students call "*agapē*-love" is the motivation of Christian education.

Because man is a dependent creature, he cannot be placed at the center of the educational process. Inescapably we come back to the idea of the ellipse: God and man and the interaction between them.

Further, the Christian educator should know what is in man in general and in individuals. To know what is in man is to understand that the downward drag of redeemed men and the perverted wills of unredeemed men will again and again thwart and block the great and noble efforts of men to build Utopia. Original sin is a factor in life that we dare not ignore, either in social planning, in the life of the church, or in the life of the individual Christian.

The wise Christian educator will "accentuate the positive and eliminate the negative." He will not be a shallow optimist or a cynical pessimist but a realist. He will steadily emphasize the positive life; he will realize that Jesus came that man might have life abundant, rich, full, and joyous. He will teach human beings to *affirm* life—to rejoice always because they have found life so gloriously meaningful in Christ. He will be a lover of men who seeks to mediate grace and forgiveness and understanding rather than a perpetual scolder of weak and frail folk. To know what is in man means to have a deep understanding of human frailty and sin, and to bear the burdens of one's fellows.

Biblically speaking, man, made in God's image, is dependent upon his Maker, responsible to his Maker, rebellious against his Maker, and redeemed through his Maker's only-begotten Son. Against this background, let us look at what psychology and the social sciences tell us about the persons we teach.

1. *Man is a unit,* a whole, a center of power who lives in relationship with other centers of power. We must, therefore, deal

with man as a living whole. We do not teach a boy's mind, or his
body, or his will, or his emotions; we teach the whole boy. It is
not enough to try to teach something to be memorized by the
brain. We are not interested simply in transmitting facts or even
in discussing ideas. We are interested in facts and ideas and attitudes and actions that accompany or grow out of the ideas. The
whole teaching process takes cognizance of the fact that man is a
total being. We teach living beings, and each one has mind, spirit,
attitudes, emotions, and body. We teach each one therefore as a
total person, not simply as a brilliant mind, a stodgy, dull person,
a slow thinker, or just an average, mediocre person. And we know
that the springs of life are in the emotions more often than in the
reason. Christian education, then, cannot deal with the transmis-
sion of mental concepts alone. We communicate the Christian
religion to the whole person.

Pushing this concept of the unity of personality a little farther,
if man is a whole, it is also true that Christianity deals with the
whole man and it deals with him in all his relationships. We do
not deal with the soul or spirit of man on Sunday only. We deal
with a boy, knowing that this boy will go to school on weekdays
and to the neighborhood picture show on Friday night and to the
ball game on Saturday afternoon. The Christianity we teach
ought to be made meaningful and relevant to all areas of life.
Genuine communication involves bringing the lad and the gospel
and the life problem into an encounter wherein the gospel comes
alive and helps the lad to solve his problem.

Man is one, a unit, a whole. The popular way to speak of man
is as a creature with a body and soul, and some would add with a
spirit. The Bible, however, pictures man just as does modern
psychology, as a whole being, a total personality. We speak popu-
larly of "every human soul," or of "saving souls." The Bible's
emphasis is not on saving souls but on saving persons. Biblically,
man does not have a soul, man *is* a soul. When the Christian
thinks of man as a unit, he thinks of a psychophysical unity, a
body-soul who is neither body nor soul but body-soul who will
have permanency, eternal life. Unlike Greek philosophy, which
spoke of the emprisoned soul being released from the body upon
death, the Christian faith speaks of the eternal unity of body and
soul. This is the meaning of the phrase in the Apostles' Creed, "in
the resurrection of the body." (See I Cor., ch. 15.) Popular Chris-

tian theology has often been more Greek than Biblical at this
point. The Bible teaches us that man is a living soul. He is a
spirit made for communion with the Eternal Spirit. In the last
few years Biblical theologians have made intensive study of the
various key words of the Bible. Some of these studies have been
of the words that indicate personality as a whole or in certain
aspects, such as flesh, body, spirit, soul, heart, and mind. The conclusion is almost unanimous that the Biblical concept of man is
much like that of modern psychology, namely, that man is a
psychophysical organism. Man is a unitary being. The Bible, of
course, goes beyond psychology in recognizing that this unitary
being is never alone but always in relationships, the primary and
supremely essential relationship being that with his Maker.

When we teach this living being, we teach him as a being who
is soul, who is body, who is spirit, who is a self. He is both a being
and a becoming. The persons we teach are units capable of living
and behaving in certain ways, unified by the fact that they are
beings who are in process of becoming what they want to become,
or what society molds them to become, or what God purposes for
them. Our task is to bring the gospel to bear upon these persons
in such a way as to help them to find and to fulfill God's will for
them.

2. *Man is a growing being.* He not only *is,* he is *becoming.* To
teach effectively another person we must know what stage of
growth that other has reached. The four-year-old girl, the four-
teen-year-old adolescent, and the forty-year-old woman are in different stages of development, and the effective teacher is aware of
those stages and speaks to those stages in proper fashion. This
means that if we are teaching a primary class, we will use language, words, teaching methods, Scripture passages that are different from those we would use if we were teaching senior high
students. There are some things a Christian family can learn together, and there are times when the whole church family ought
to have learning experiences together. But people do grow, and
gradation is an inescapable fact. We use graded literature, have
proper age groupings, with age group projects and occasional age
group worship. We have to try to understand our people as they
are at their particular ages. There are some fundamental traits of
each age group, and we have to learn those traits as we work with
that given age group. Today most denominational programs of

Christian education include articles, pamphlets, or books that give
guidance to teachers concerning the characteristics and developmental needs and particular problems of the age which they are
teaching. Much of this helpful material is included in the regular
literature prepared for the teacher of a given age group, or in the
parent-teacher quarterlies in such a curriculum as that of The
United Presbyterian Church in the U.S.A.

In speaking of growth, psychologists tend to use the word "maturity." Man grows to maturity. But there are levels of maturity.
A mature ten-year-old would not be mature in the sense that a
fifty-year-old is mature. Further, there is no such thing as perfect
maturity within the reach of mortal man. Some folk become relatively mature; others seem to remain relatively immature even
though chronologically quite old; but perfect maturity is beyond
us. The psychologist as he speaks of maturity does not necessarily
mean what the Christian means when he uses the word. The psychologist is likely to think that a man who has a really mature
mind has all the resources he needs within himself, that he can
live independently of any other, whereas the Christian will think,
Man can never be so mature as to be independent of God. H. A.
Overstreet, in his popular book *The Mature Mind* (W. W.
Norton & Company, Inc., 1949), was stating the naturalistic and
not the Christian understanding of maturity when he deplored
the fact that some religions "insist upon the permanent childlike
dependence of man upon an all-powerful and all-commanding
Deity" (*ibid.,* p. 271).

The Christian, in his concept of maturity, believes firmly in the
dignity of man, but he also unashamedly realizes that man is dependent upon the grace and mercy of God, and that man is steadily guided and empowered by the Holy Spirit. The responsible
Christian is a man who in spirit and attitude is mature in relationship to himself and his fellow men, who has a wholesome self-
respect, and who has a genuine respect and love for his fellowmen. "You shall love your neighbor as yourself." (Matt. 22:39.)
But this is not enough, for there must also be the love of God and
the dependence upon him. Man is always creature, depending
upon his Creator for sustaining grace. In Christian maturity, we
have such a deep and vital relationship to God that, surrendering
to him, we become free to be our best selves. We are "mature in
Christ." George Matheson's hymn, "Make Me a Captive, Lord,

and Then I Shall Be Free," expresses this truth beautifully. It is
not childish immaturity but childlike wisdom to be dependent
upon God. Our Calvinistic ancestors were right when they
shouted, "Fear God—and fear no man!"

The Christian accepts the psychological concept of growth or
becoming or development. All normal people grow in various
aspects of their beings, as well as in a total sense. Growth is not
automatic, nor is it steady and continuous. Not only do persons
differ in rates of growth, but each person also has different rates
of growth for various aspects of his being. Often growth goes
steadily along for a while, then has spurts, major or minor.
Growth in any aspect of life, including one's spiritual life and
one's relationships with others, is not steadily upward. It is more
likely to be a stair-step, or an ascending spiral that winds back
upon itself from time to time. Our tendency to sin is responsible,
of course, for the fact that we do not grow steadily and consist-
ently all through life. Even the most dedicated Christian will slip
back a bit and have to make up ground on his life's journey.

3. *Man is a social being.* Robinson Crusoe on a desert island
was not the true symbol of man, nor was Symeon Stylites, on the
desert pillar, removed from his fellow men, and spending his time
in worship of God. Man is a social being meant for fellowship
with other human beings and to a large extent dependent upon
others. Each person takes on some of the coloration of his character and his personality from the society in which he grows up.

Augustine long ago spoke of the mass of sin of which we are a
part and which becomes a part of us. The cultural anthropologists
have taught us how powerfully the influences of society play upon
and help to mold the growing person. All that we have met is a
part of us. We are the creatures of our homes and schools and
culture. Now this is not the whole truth about man, for Christian
theology suggests that it is the inner man and not the outer conditions that finally is determinative of a man's destiny. But socio-
logical conditions color decidedly the thinking and the feeling of
people, so that the whole process of teaching is to a considerable
extent dependent upon the background of the people with whom
we would communicate. Our teaching is dependent upon the
kind of culture in which we live. We cannot teach an Eskimo that
Jesus is the lamb of God, for an Eskimo has never seen a lamb.
It would be a meaningless concept to him. He would understand,

however, if we were to say, "Jesus is the baby seal of God." Our wiser missionaries long ago learned that the Bible has to be translated into words people can understand, for we are the children of our cultures.

The Christian would say that man is determined largely by the society in which he lives and to a lesser degree by his heredity, but that man is always a responsible being, free, at least within limits, to make his own choices. Man feels himself to be responsible for his own acts and attitudes. Environment and heredity have a great deal to say about what we become, yet in the end it is the inner being, the self, which determines finally what we are and what we do.

4. *Individuals differ*. This is almost the first thing one learns if one is going to be a teacher. Each person is a unique individual with characteristics that mark him as being different from each other person. We have to learn to treat all human beings as individuals who differ. We must learn to respect those differences, even if they are peculiar!

Because of the enormous importance of this principle, let us develop it a bit. Individual differences cannot be understood without recognizing that individuality grows out of a common humanity.

a. *In some ways all human beings are alike*. They are conceived by the sex act, they dwell for nine months of amazing growth in a sheltered, symbiotic existence in their mother's womb. They undergo a real and often traumatic experience as they pass through the birth canal and out into the cold, cruel world. Life in this world is begun for them with a spank and a cry. Then they grow and develop and maturate. They are hungry and eat. They are thirsty and drink. They are weaned. They learn sphincter and bladder control. They learn to love and be loved, or they learn to distrust life. They learn to get along with people or they become afraid of people. They start to school. They reach puberty and become puzzled and puzzling adolescents. They struggle with sex and the moral code. They fall in love and probably marry. They choose a vocation, or more likely, fall into one blindly. They have children and become middle-aged, reach their peak, or fail to reach it, and sooner or later, they die. And from the first cry to the last faint breath, they live life under God. All human beings are alike. They laugh, they cry; they run, they play; they lose their temper and they are sorry. They are tempted and sometimes they fall. They pray or wish they knew how to pray. In some ways all human beings of all ages are alike. Time does not change the fundamental needs of human beings. The deepest of all needs continues to be, in the words of Augustine, "Thou hast made us for thyself, O God, and our hearts are restless until they find their rest in thee." We know that these things naturally happen to normal human beings. We have all gone through these experiences, though the nature of these experiences has been differently perceived.

b. *Some human beings are like some other human beings.* Francis Schmidt, former coach at Ohio State, when his team was to play Notre Dame while the "Fighting Irish" were at their very best, said to them, "There is no need to be scared of Notre Dame, they put on their pants one leg at a time just like you do." And this is it! All males are alike. Even so we can say: all schoolteachers are alike, all movie stars are alike, all teen-agers are alike—having a genuine subculture of their own. This is true, but it isn't the whole truth. They are alike but yet unique. If we are teaching high school young people, we have to know they have their own culture. Even though they live in the midst of a fairly clear-cut culture for their part of the country, they have their own particular attitudes and actions and habits. The subculture of high school youth in Los Angeles is not precisely like the subculture in Louisville. In fact, in a large city there may be several high school subcultures with each high school producing a recognizable patterned type. We have to know what they are like *in our community.* All teen-agers are alike, and yet we also have to add "if they live in Louisville," or "if they live in Los Angeles." But even this is not the whole truth, because we can take eight or ten teenagers in any high school in Louisville, and each one is different.

c. *In some ways no human being is like any other human being.* Each man is a unique individual, and we have to know him as such. If we have ten children in a class, each child is different from each other child. He has different points of sensitivity, different thresholds of understanding, different reaction speeds, different levels at which he may be tempted, different levels at which he may be challenged. Because each person is unique, one could theorize that we ought to have a different teacher for each learner. This would be absurd, for there are some great values in the social nature of man. But we do have to take the fact of individual differences seriously.

We ought to know within reason the ways in which all human beings are alike, and the ways in which members of a given vocation, class, age group, sex, or subculture are alike. More important, we have to know that each individual is unique, and we ought to try to understand his particular uniqueness. Many teachers fail at one or more of these points, particularly with regard to the fact that persons differ. A good teacher understands his class well enough after a while to know that he has to make this kind of approach for Tom and that kind of approach for Mary and yet another kind for Johnny. He has a little for each in a given lesson, or perhaps he will stress this angle one session and the next time that, but he does try to deal with the uniqueness of his class as well as with the ways in which they are alike.

There are some fundamental human needs to which the church must minister, needs to which the gospel speaks. The most significant of these needs are: to be whole or healthy; to love and to be loved; to feel needed; to feel of worth; to have some significance in life, to have success occasionally; to fail from time to time; to win a little praise; and to live in tension and in conflict. (Only the near dead are without tension or conflict. Too much tension results in high blood pressure or in ulcers, while too little tension may suggest a door-mat type.) The deepest need of all is for God. At the functional level, these are the dynamic, driving needs of persons. The church and the family must help people to find Christian answers to these deep inner needs. Through our living and our teaching, we should give them experiences of having these needs answered. In the teaching process it is particularly important for the children to know that the teacher is really concerned for them as persons of worth.

Some Developmental Needs of Human Beings

In recent years the psychologists have studied intensively if not exhaustively the various ages of life. They have set forth for us the norms of growth and development for each age and have listed some of the main psychological needs at each stage for the developing human being. The curriculum experts make use of these findings in their work. Church school leaders can also make use of some of these findings. We conclude this chapter with a somewhat sketchy listing of these main needs at some key stages.

Barring unfortunate prenatal influences, such as German measles, the baby will probably come into the world with reasonable health, and we hope, wanted and accepted. From birth on there are random movements. Only gradually does the child learn to know hand from foot. In time he realizes that when he scratches this way he scratches his own face. Then he begins to reach out and scratch somebody else's face! The baby learns gradually and individually the parts of his own body, and eventually he learns to co-ordinate the actions of these parts. He develops from a random, diffused state of everything moving at once to a gradual ability to move each part separately as he wishes. As he matures, he develops a new kind of unity, unity of personality, structure, and character.

In the first year of life, the process of growth is about as follows: at three months, he smiles; around the fourth month, he stops crying when he hears steps at feeding time. In the fourth or fifth month, he plays peekaboo, beginning in a vague sort of way to get some sense of identity. The feedings are quite important. We know now that children desperately need to be held in the mother's arms, even if she cannot breast-feed. The baby needs some cuddling. In fact, unless the baby receives some love, some emotional warmth, he is in danger of growing up to be a person who can never relate warmly to others. In the first year, then, the child must receive tender, loving care. He also must gain a basic sense of trust, which comes to him from love and from consistency of treatment, so that his physical wants and needs are met with regularity (not of an arbitrary chart in a book but according to his personal nature).

Between twelve months and thirty-six months, the child becomes a relatively independent person. He begins to know himself as a person and to gain autonomy. The dawning sense of initiative is important. "Me do!" he rightly insists. Around two and a half, his favorite words are "no" and "I won't!" As the months pass, he becomes more positive even as he moves steadily toward autonomy. If in this period he is shamed too much, he gets an inferiority complex and seldom gets over it. Later, psychiatrists can help him live with it, but they are not likely to cure him. During what the psychologists call "the battle of the potty" the child is taught sphincter and bladder control. If the mother is too harsh, the child may feel greatly shamed. We try therefore to teach him self-control without loss of self-esteem. We want him to become an autonomous person, knowing himself as a person, so what he must gain in this period is independence without shame. "I am a person, and I don't have to be ashamed of myself as a person." "I like me." The first three years are largely spent at home, but the nursery class teachers get the child in the second or third year, and they too have the important responsibility of accepting the child as a person and of helping him to feel confident as a human being.

In the fourth and fifth years, the child develops a conscience. There were faint glimmerings of one earlier, but in these years conscience comes alive. The child begins to feel guilty when he does something he should not do. He begins to differentiate between right and wrong. If he develops too strong a sense of guilt in the four to five stage, he may go through life overly rigid in his personality. Parents and teachers should encourage his initiative, give him lots of freedom, should avoid stressing the sense of guilt too strongly, and should teach him the meaning of forgiveness.

During the primary and junior years, from six through eleven, the child goes to school, meets the outside world in a new and broadening way, and learns to associate with all kinds of children. The beginning year at school is most important. If he learns to read quickly and well, he has a good chance of enjoying the realm of knowledge. During these years of steady growth, the child gradually learns the sense of duty, the joy of accomplishment, fair play, and co-operation. The junior years, nine to eleven, are particularly delightful for the teacher, for the child is usually friendly and eager, and if he is rightly motivated, he can learn more quickly and remember better than at any other stage. If the teacher has caught his loyalty and affection, he is likely to learn much, but if he is treated unfairly or harshly, he may become bitter and resentful. This is the best of all periods to stress the memorization of great passages of the Bible. The junior child will gain a respectable knowledge of the Bible; he loves the great Biblical stories and Jesus Christ. He may show a fine Christian spirit in his attitudes. But do not expect him to stay still!

Ages twelve to sixteen, the time of puberty and adolescence, constitute an extremely important period of life. The child of this age in most societies has certain major functions to carry out.

He has to become psychologically weaned from his parents. This is the primary reason for the intensity of his feelings on occasion. Due to the biological changes, he is not quite certain whether he is a child or an adult, and neither are his parents. In the midst of this uncertainty, emotions may and do flare up occasionally. The Germans used to call adolescence the period of storm and stress. It still is in many a home. The child *must* become independent of his parents, and this is never easy. During this period the child is more concerned with what other people think of him than he is with anything else. He has his radar screeens up, his antennae are out, he is sending and receiving the wave lengths of his peers. "What do they think of me? Am I accepted by the crowd?"

The adolescent, of course, also has to accept himself as a mature sexual being. These powerful new forces within, this entrancing fact that he is physically an adult, and the tragic fact that often he has been given no sex education of merit combine to make the adjustment to a mature male or female role one that is difficult. Particularly is this true in our kind of society. The church has a rich opportunity to work with parents and to supplement what parents have done by way of sex education. The church should help its youth to face some of the very real sex problems of high school youth in the light of the Christian view of sex and love and marriage.

Adolescents have to learn how to get along with others in groups and as individuals. They have to make the fundamental life decisions:

What shall be my lifework?

What shall be my life philosophy (religion)?

Whom shall I marry?

With regard to these, and all other major problems of the adolescent, the church should face with them the light the Christian gospel casts upon these areas of life. Further, during these years the child of the covenant should be led to confirm the covenant vows for himself and become a communing member of the church. Adolescents in churches that do not practice infant baptism should be led to make their decision for Christ and to join the church. These are indeed crucial years from the religious standpoint, for they are the years of the basic decisions.

True enough, the choice of a lifemate usually comes after this period is over. Between seventeen and twenty-one the adolescent develops a deep sense of intimacy with a few others. He now knows well who he is as a real person. He understands himself fairly well, he loves himself and his fellows, and he may have a genuine and enthusiastic love of Christ. His sense of intimacy becomes involved with a member of the opposite sex in real earnestness toward the end of the period. Trouble here in accepting and controlling his sexuality and his role as male or female is real trouble. From about twenty for the female and twenty-three for the male, love is the key word, and shortly he marries.

We lack sufficient space to continue the story in detail. The very young adult who is married has to adjust to being a married person, and then in time to parenthood. He is on the march to success in his chosen occupation, or he is engaged in graduate or professional training. He has an urge to creativity and a wish to be genuinely mature. He takes on adult responsibilities and assumes important tasks and obligations. In adulthood he has to gain and live out a sense of integrity in attitude and action. In the middle years of life it is a case of "now or never." For many a person, the year forty marks failure; for by then he knows he will never reach the peak to which he had aspired. He may become sour or embittered, or he may take life in stride, or he may learn through the power of the Holy Spirit to take what life brings of good and ill, of fulfillment and of disappointment, of joy and of sorrow, to face life with triumph and peace and joy. As old age comes on, a man begins to realize that a lot of things he used to worry about are not so important after all. He simplifies his ideals, his attitudes, his actions, and centers on those things which now seem most important. The normal, mature old person does this, but some seem to decay instead. The Christian faith in the middle years of life can be a marvelous source of "strength for the journey," and in the later years of life it can cast the light of eternity on the end of the road and can enable a man to look to the end with grateful anticipation.

How to Teach This Lesson

1. The lesson could be introduced by the filmstrip *No Two Alike.* (*The Leadership Education Audio-Visual Kit.*) Then discuss its meaning for Christian teaching.

2. Have a summary lecture by the teacher, then talks by various

members or guest leaders on the characteristics of each age group.

3. If a competent Christian psychologist is available, have him and the teacher and the minister serve as a panel-forum to discuss the Christian view of man.

4. Much of modern literature sees man as an animal; much of scientific literature sees man as an aspiring ape; much of communist literature sees man as an ant; much of idealistic literature sees man as an angel. What does the Biblical view of man say to these ideas?

5. Research reports could be made on the use of various significant Bible words such as "body," "spirit," etc., or on Paul's view of man, Jesus' view of man, etc.

VII

How We Learn

We have discussed the foundations of Christian education, the Bible as the textbook of the Christian community, the church as the covenant community, the church and the family as nurturing communities that together share the responsibility of teaching and living and passing on the Christian faith. We have looked at the nature of man as revealed in the Bible and in the social sciences. We have seen that encounter—being confronted by the presence of the living God, meeting the Master face to face—is the heart of Christian education. In the divine-human encounter, we are changed.

Learning is change. There is no teaching unless there is learning, and there is no learning unless there is change. This means not only the change that comes from more knowledge, but also change of attitude, change in ways of believing, thinking, perceiving, acting, doing. In Christian education we seek to have changes take place as a result of the teaching-learning process. We want those whom we teach to change in the direction of Christlikeness. Persons do not become more Christlike except as they come to know Christ as Lord and Savior and grow by grace and by the work and power of the Holy Spirit into his likeness, so that the Christian who is growing is the one who is in Christ.

In the experiences we call Christian education, the changes that take place are of all sorts, from the acquisition of more information to the developing of broad concepts of Christian faith, from the acquisition of skill in Christian living to the development of fundamental life attitudes.

The changes take place in us and in our ways of looking at things. The Bible does not change, but our understanding of its

91

facts and their meanings may change. God does not change, but as we come into relationship with him, we change. The changes take place at various levels within us, but the deepest changes take place in the spirit of man, in the self.

Some Background Concerning Learning

Human beings are so made that they cannot help learning. In fact, most of us want to learn. But we do not want to learn everything. We want to learn only those things in which we have an interest, those things in which we have become involved, those things which have caught us up and have moved us deeply. We feel more intensely the value of learning some things than we do other things. Most children have real difficulty learning history because they do not see the relevance of history to their own lives. Teen-age boys who have never been used to books around the house usually have difficulty sensing the value of reading the classics of the Christian faith. "Why go to the trouble of studying the catechism? I can't understand all those big words anyhow."

Human beings are so made that they are bound to learn. We cannot live without learning—something, at least. But it is axiomatic, since John Dewey, that *interest* is one of the basic keys to the learning process. It is very difficult to learn when we are not interested and do not see the reason for studying this or learning that. Help a pupil to become interested in a subject, and he is far more likely to learn it.

We learn more rapidly and more effectively and more joyfully when we are truly interested. And we become interested when we become personally involved in some manner. We learn some routine things because we have to do so in order to learn something challenging. We can have something pounded into our heads long enough for us to pass an examination, but this is not true learning. We learn best, not when a teacher tries to force us or to entice us to learn, but when we are so involved and so interested that we get caught up and lose ourselves in the learning task. The normal teen-age boy has no trouble being motivated to engage in a varsity sport if he has athletic ability; the normal pre-adolescent girl has no difficulty learning to dance; the soldier who knows he is going into combat learns readily the life-preserving tricks that are taught him, whereas a young man in peacetime may find it difficult to keep his mind on such seemingly irrelevant knowledge. The church school teacher wisely endeavors to involve actively class members in the teaching-learning process.

Pupils learn when they want to learn. When they set up a mental block against learning, it is practically impossible to teach them. When a junior high school lad thinks that football is all-important but Latin is for the birds, he is not going to do well in Latin. When a class of juniors in church school thinks that "we are studying the same old stuff, we have heard these stories before," the class is not likely to grow spiritually. Real learning, after early childhood, takes place only where there is interest, involvement, the desire to learn. For learning to occur, there must be acceptance of the teacher, of the learning situation, of the material (content, project "lesson") and of oneself as learner *now*.

When one is rightly and highly motivated, learning comes naturally and more easily. As a friend who wanted to enroll for a graduate course in Christian education said: "I now know I am weak in this field. I have just got to learn more about it. I'm really ready to work." That man will learn!

The teacher has the responsibility of helping pupils to gain interest and to become motivated to learn. It is the task of the teacher to help the pupil to grasp the meaning and relevance of the Bible stories. The pupil needs to know not simply what the story says but also what the story means. What did it mean to those who participated in it? What does it mean to me as I identify myself with the characters and live through this story again? How does God's word speak to me through these ancient words? When he starts to ask these questions, he is ready to learn.

In Christian education, then, we do not think it is sufficient to tell boys and girls, men and women, the facts of the Bible. It is not enough to teach them that once upon a time Moses led the children of Israel out of Egypt; we must help them to understand the meaning of this great historic event, and why it is referred to to again and again in the Bible, as a symbol of God's dealing with his people, of his redemption of his people from the bondage of sin. We interpret this great event; we try to make it come alive and be meaningful to persons living today. This story is just a bit of ancient history, which merely adds to our store of information, until its meaning comes alive and then we experience changes

within as we grasp the might and the grace of the God who redeems his people from bondage.

One of the key words in modern psychology is the term "perception." We are just beginning to understand that we learn
what we perceive, not what we fail to perceive. If we do not see
it, we cannot get it. In a class of ten junior highs, it may be that
three will be mature enough to share the teacher's perception of
what is involved in the temptation of Jesus, while the other seven
students perceive the story on an immature level and are bored
by the class hour. We perceive facts and meanings on the basis
of past experiences. Our native equipment, our heredity, plus our
experiences as we have grown up in our particular environments,
largely determine what we perceive. It is the whole man who
learns, and he learns what he is ready to learn.

One of the chief goals of Christian education is to help Christians perceive all moral problems, all issues of life, all decision-
demanding situations, from the perspective of the Christian faith.
But we gain this Christian perspective only as we have growing
experiences of the Christian faith. We build on our past knowledge and experiences in learning of Christ just as we do in learning anything else. But the Holy Spirit is a never-to-be-forgotten
factor in Christian learning.

"We learn to do by doing." This is one of the most vital of all
principles of learning. Some things are taught by the telling-listen-
ing process. But the more vital things are usually taught through
dynamic processes of personal experience. We learn to do by activity, by participation, by doing. A minister best learns to preach
not by reading a textbook on preaching but by preaching. The
hiatus is not so sharp for, of course, one both reads and acts. But
reading without accompanying practice or experience is usually
a poor teacher. The whole nature of professional education—law,
medicine, ministry, etc.—is changing by virtue of this principle.
Once ministers spent three years studying the theories of religion,
then went out, green, to begin to serve. Today ministerial students
carry on an active program of field service or field education as
part of their program of study. Principle and practice go together.

In the Sunday church school the pupils learn best by doing,
even as they do in public school. We learn the meaning of religion through religious practices and through having experiences
of the religious life. Boys and girls learn to pray, for instance, not

simply by reading a passage in the Bible about prayer, but also by observing others lead corporate prayer, by entering into corporate prayer, by working with their classmates to write a prayer, by haltingly praying in public once and again and yet again. Through active participation one learns what it means to live as a Christian in a group. You can verbalize, "God is faithful," but you can learn this only as in your own experience you live in trust and find that God keeps his promises.

It is possible to enter vicariously into the experience of others, and one can experience some Christian truths by identifying oneself with a Biblical character and going through the experience with him that is recorded in the Bible. Because of the reality of this principle of participation, we find that simple religious drama, spontaneously produced by a class, is one of the best teaching methods. The present use of role-playing is another indication of the value of this principle of vicarious activity.

We learn, then, on the basis of our past experience, of our personality structure and our ways of living and of perceiving, and we learn effectively when we are interested and motivated, and when we can engage in creative activities.

Some Learning Theories

The educational world has not yet reached a definitive theory of how we learn. Let us look briefly at some learning theories, each of which has some truth in it. Christian educators make use of all these theories within limits.

Possibly the most prominent learning theory is that of the conditioned response. In its simple form we say we learn by practice. A classic experiment by a Russian scientist about 1905 was the impetus for the modern emphasis on this idea of learning by conditioning. When Pavlov's famous dog was shown a piece of meat, the saliva naturally would come, for the dog was getting ready to eat and digest the meat. Pavlov began to feed the dog in a specific way. He would ring a bell, then give the meat. After a while, when he rang the bell, without giving the meat, the salivary glands would begin to function. The dog had been conditioned so that his salivary glands would function with the ringing of the bell. This story of the dog and the bell and the piece of meat is probably known to everyone who has ever studied psychology. From it modern behavioristic psychology took its start. The ringing bell is the conditioned stimulus. Given the stimulus, the desired response follows. This is learning by conditioning or training.

The theory goes that this is the way we human beings learn. Obviously this theory puts us on purely an animal level. Dogs and other animals can be conditioned. The theory perfectly describes specific items and aspects of learning by rats and cats and rabbits in a laboratory. It also describes the way the human infant learns. The baby learns in its experiences of faithfulness and regularity, of doing the same thing in the same way at the same time(s) day after day, that life has its rules and its stated times for eating and bathing and sleeping. While few parents would be satisfied to say that they teach their babies just as they train their dogs, it is true up to a point. Most of our basic habits, our routine practices, and our skills are learned by conditioning or training. So are many of our tastes. It is likely that underlying all learning are the basic habits and skills to which we have been conditioned. There is no learning without conditioning, but learning cannot be described entirely by the conditioning theory.

Simple religious habits are learned by the conditioning process. Reverence, the habit of prayer, the habit of daily Bible-reading, and the habit of church attendance are so learned. It is folly to scorn these simple habits. On the Sabbath Day, Jesus, as his custom was, went into the synagogue (Luke 4:16). Church and family should unite in giving these good habits to their members.

Some people, whether parents or teachers, believe that we can condition people by punishment. We learn to do this because we are punished if we fail to do it; we learn not to do that lest we be punished if we do. To a very limited degree we do learn by punishment. But it is a poor method of training human beings, as any child psychologist or criminologist can tell you. We learn more by praise than we do by punishment. One of Thorndike's laws of learning was the law of satisfaction or reward. We learn those things which are rewarding to learn. Animal training is largely based on this concept of training, by reward and punishment. But no man learns the love of God this way. A person cannot be trained to be good, though he can be trained to be careful. A person cannot be trained to be a great musician, though he can be trained mechanically to play great music.

At this point in our writing came the shout from the street,

"There it is!" And out we rushed to join the neighbors as all the street gathered to watch the balloon satellite Echo I cross the Louisville sky. The thought came to us: A man cannot be *trained* to do the kind of thinking that put the satellite up in the sky. Other learning methods certainly helped. With all due respect to Pavlov, Sputnik did not get into orbit merely by dint of skillful conditioning on the part of Russian scientists. Brilliant inventiveness, adventuresome thinking, and the problem-solving techniques are not simply the products of conditioning or habit.

The conditioning theory is true as far as it goes, but it is not adequate to explain the kinds of learning we do in adolescence or in adulthood. Much learning comes not simply by training given to one, but rather by the active will of persons who want to learn, by the whole personality responding alertly and eagerly to the total learning situation.

Another major form of learning theory is known as trial and error, or as some prefer, trial and success. We try things out for size and finally we find that which fits. Children learn this way, and so do adults in some areas of life. Perhaps the most important type of trial-and-error learning, as far as we are concerned in Christian education, is what is known as problem-solving. John Dewey, in discussing how we think, made the wise observation that we learn through conscious effort to overcome difficulty. We learn when we are motivated but blocked. Then we try hard, and we learn to get around the block and reach our goal. Dewey's problem-solving technique ran something like this: There is a difficulty, and we are aware of it. We go through the process of making specific to ourselves what the difficulty is. We think through alternative ways of meeting and overcoming the difficulty. We see what will probably work to get us out of this spot. We may search for further information. Then we probably frame a hypothesis: I believe this is the way we will get out of the difficulty. Then we try it out to see. This is the way we think, the way we resolve our problems, the way we learn. But what has just been written is a very simple description of what may be a very complicated process. This procedure is closely akin to the heart of the scientific method.

Dewey's contribution has been of great value in Christian education. We set projects and problems for our boys and girls in Sunday church school. Or better still we help them to get into problem situations in which they have to live out certain attitudes to see what is good and what is bad, what is Christian and what is unchristian. We teach by dramatics and by role-playing. We teach by having youth and adults discuss problems, analyze situations, look for possible solutions, and test out the solutions.

We learn through problem-solving because we are involved, we are challenged, the best that is in us is drawn out in the effort to meet the challenge. With this general approach to learning, we start with the problem and turn to the Bible and other resources to help with the solution. This is not the only way of learning, but it is a dynamic and valuable way. We learn through problem-solving activities how the gospel can apply to the social and moral issues of the day.

One of the most significant theories of learning is that we learn by insight. Both Gestalt psychology (the psychology that deals with patterns or wholes or configurations and therefore with relationships) and field psychology, which deals with fields of force that play upon the individual in any given situation, teach us that we learn primarily at higher levels through insight. We learn not simply by conditioning, nor even by trial and error, though both are involved always. We also learn by grasping the whole, by leaps of reason, by an intuitive grasp of the nature of the solution. "Eureka, I have found it!" Archimedes is reputed to have shouted as he ran naked into the street from his tub to tell the world that he had discovered the principle of specific gravity. The insight approach to learning is the concept that we discover suddenly what the answer is. We've wrestled with it, we've thought about it, but we haven't seen any answer, then suddenly the light flashes and we know the answer. We do learn this way.

Such insight does not come in a vacuum. 'Way down beneath the surface there are habit patterns involved, which are conditioned reflexes. Insight comes only after various tries have been made to solve the problem in one way or another. Then suddenly the pieces fall into a pattern, the relationships are discerned, and the answer is seen. Many important scientific discoveries have come in this manner. In a few instances the insight has come in a dream but only after much intensive work, experimenting, seeking the answer.

One suspects that the leap of imagination which is new insight into the Christian faith is most likely to come during a Communion service or during a sermon. But such leaps may come when a class is discussing seriously the meaning for today of some great Biblical passage. Without solid study somewhere along the line leaps are not likely to take place. This solid study, this active, class-involved approach is essential if there is to be real learning.

In the Christian faith there is a place for teaching by drill and by rote memory. We teach little children some things largely by conditioning processes, but other things are taught largely by way of relationships in situations. At adolescent and adult levels, learning by way of relationship in situations is common. We have been talking about the relationship of the gospel to life. We have talked about the relationship of the person to himself, to others, and supremely to God. Through the varied relationships of life, and insight into these relationships, people learn. We have many Christian experiences in which we learn by leaps of the imagination, by insight, by a grasping of the significance of the interrelationships of the various parts of the pattern of life—this particular pattern in which we now live.

Deeper Levels of Learning

Changes occur at deeper levels of personality, of heart and mind, as we engage in encounter with other persons and with the Lord. When a teacher confronts the class and when the class encounters the teacher, changes are going to take place if any teaching occurs. Changes in attitudes and in emotion are most likely to occur if there is exchange of ideas and points of view. Where there is real encounter, real meeting between human spirits in the presence of the Divine Spirit, changes may and often do occur. New ideas begin to explode in one's brain, new feelings move deep within one, new points of view open up, and daring new action may be taken. Where there is real encounter in a class, changes may take place in teacher as well as in class, for never in a learning situation does just one person learn. To be a teacher is to learn.

As we learn in the Christian life, we take on new attitudes toward our fellow men and toward the problems of life. We are likely to become less dogmatic and more tolerant of human frailty, more humble and less self-righteous. As we live and grow in the Christian community of family or church, our relationships grow deeper and richer and more meaningful. The stack of chips on our shoulder diminishes greatly, and we learn to live more happily with others because we have learned what it is to be part of the *koinōnia*, a participant in the family of God. These changes that take place within us do not all come at once. We continue to grow in Christian knowledge, in Christian understanding, in Christian love, and not least in Christian faith. Our joy is more genuine, our courage to accept ourselves more profound, our hope more certain as the years pass and we have more and more, deeper and deeper meetings with our fellows *in Christ*. Ever and always we need to remember that these changes which take place in our human relationships, these deeper insights into human personality, this growing ability to accept our fellowmen as they are and not try to remold them in our own image, this deepening compassion, this wisdom about life, come about in a community in which the Spirit of God is present and participant. He partakes of the inner action between the selves in the fellowship that is the church.

And we never get away from the primary encounter between man and God, between the person and the Person. Lewis Sherrill says, "As man encounters God, the nature of the responses which the human self makes to the divine self indicates the nature of the changes taking place in the depths of the self" (*op. cit.*, p. 157).

The changes that take place in our relationships with our fellow men ultimately grow out of the changes that take place within us as a result of the divine-human encounter. The self is confronted by the living God not once only, but again and again. From infancy on, the individual meets his Maker as he pilgrimages. The mature Christian may meet God daily, perhaps many times a day, in such an encounter that a "yes" or "no" is necessary. There is not just one encounter, one "yes" to God. How often we meet God is in part dependent on the number of times that we are tempted, the number of problems that confront us, the number of decisions we have to make, the number of opportunities that open up before us. Sherrill points out that while the Bible says something about conversion, it says a great deal more about repentance. Repentance is a change of mind (in the sense of basic attitudes of personality), and repentance may well be a daily affair.

We change as we are converted, and there is a sense in which we may be converted bit by bit even as we repent bit by bit. Many a Christian in the South, for instance, is deeply and wholesomely

Christian, yet because he is a human being he has taken on the coloration of his society, and in his attitude toward the race question he may well need to be converted. Nor is this limited to the South! Such conversion, or such repentance if you prefer, is not going to be enforced by law or by intimidation but must come from within. This is in the sphere of relationships and changes needed can come only in that sphere. The Alabama girl who sent word to us half-jestingly, "Greetings from a magnolia blossom who is dying but still fighting," is changing more than she knows. Some millions of others need to be penitent concerning the nerve that leads to the pocketbook. The nationalist in his ebullient pride also needs to repent. And the good people need to read often the story of the elder brother (Luke, ch. 15). When we confront our brethren in Christ on these various issues, we may gradually change. Usually the change is gradual; sometimes the change, the new learning, the conversion, comes almost instantaneously. In the poem *The Everlasting Mercy,* John Masefield's description of Saul Kane's conversion offers a brilliant study of such sudden change. The drunkard's self-centeredness was burned alive by the deep peace of the Spirit; the barriers were down and he was free from the shackles of sin; and he knew that by the grace of Christ he had been reborn in order to be a brother to all men. Another and better-known Saul also underwent a dramatic transformation on the Damascus road, when he met his Master face to face (Acts 9:1-9). Such sudden changes of course have antecedents. Nevertheless, the change is so deep and so great, and seemingly so sudden, that Christians have used such picture language as conversion, a new birth, a new creation, a new man, to describe the experience. "Regeneration," the theologian calls it. This word covers the ultimate commitment of the self to its Maker. Born anew! The whole concept of the covenant community implies that not all Christians undergo this experience suddenly and dramatically. For many, it may well be gradual. But all Christians undergo, again and again, the experience of repentance, which involves a change of mind in the sense of a deep change in the way one views life, a change that touches the will and affects one's conduct. Always the downward drag of sin is with us, and always we need the grace of God.

Theologically as well as psychologically, learning is a matter of insight and relationship and encounter and change. And the

supreme relationship of life is that with God. When we encounter
him, we change. To say no to him is to change, to change in the
wrong, the negative direction. To say yes to God is to be changed
in a wholesome, positive, affirmative direction. The one deep and
fundamental decision of life, around which all other decisions
cluster, is the ultimate "yes" or "no" man gives to God. A man
can become a new creation in Christ if he listens to the call of
God. It is the task of the Christian educator to try to help all with
whom he works to have frequent encounters with God in which
various issues and relationships are worked through. It is the
task of the Christian church to see that every man everywhere has
a chance to accept Jesus Christ as his Lord and Savior. This is the
goal of evangelism and both the starting point and the goal of
Christian education.

The deeper changes that take place in the human self do not
take place by our own wisdom or by our own will alone, or even
by the help of our best Christian friends. If changes toward Christlikeness are to come about, the Holy Spirit must participate in
the process. And he does! In a sense, the Holy Spirit may be
present in all teaching that endeavors to help man to live effectively and nobly in this present world. But he is surely present in
all teaching that is specifically and definitely Christian. Whenever
human beings endeavor to unfold the nature and meaning of the
gospel and its implications for life, in the spirit of prayer, they
will receive some guidance from God as they teach. As teachers, we
cannot bring about the deeper changes, but we can so live and so
teach in the Christian fellowship that we can create the climate of
change. God changes us!

How to Teach This Lesson

1. A week ahead, ask each person to write on this topic: Describe how you learned to do something such as play Ping-pong,
sew, drive a car, swim, or pray. Have several of these read; discuss them, drawing forth learning principles.

2. Assign: Be prepared to tell what person has helped most to
make you what you are, and why this person has so greatly in-
fluenced you.

3. Divide your class, on the basis of choice, to work individually
on one of the following topics: How would you interest or mo-

tivate a class of senior highs to study the catechism seriously? a
class of junior highs to study the Ten Commandments? a class of
juniors to study Paul's missionary journeys? a class of primaries to
study the story of Abraham?

4. Use one of the *Leadership Education Audio-Visual Kit* filmstrips, or one of the age group filmstrips, showing how we learn.
Discuss. In an orientation class that continues for a year, the
teacher would make use of several if not all of these helpful filmstrips. The best single one for the purpose of this lesson, probably,
is entitled *How Persons Learn.*

VIII

How We Teach

Jesus has been called "the master teacher." And so he was! Universally he is listed among the great teachers of mankind. He was far more than a teacher, of course, but he truly was master of the art of teaching. He was called a great teacher because of the manner of his teaching as well as the content of his teaching. Wonderful though the content of his teaching was, it does not save us. His teaching was part of his saving work, but it is not enough by itself to bring salvation. We need more than great spiritual truths. His death and resurrection are the central facts about his life; by these he saved us. Assuming this, it is still true that he was a magnificent teacher both in what he taught and in the manner of his teaching.

It is not our purpose to discuss the content of his teaching, but the manner of it. How did Jesus teach? What was the secret of his power as a teacher?

When Nicodemus came to Jesus by night, he said, "Rabbi, we know that you are a teacher come from God" (John 3:2). One Gospel writer described his teaching thus, "And they were astonished at his teaching, for he taught them as one who had authority, and not as the scribes" (Mark 1:22).

Why was he so great a teacher? Because "he knew what was in man" (John 2:25; Matt. 9:4); because he had both love and respect for each human being as a child of God, a being of great value in God's sight, worth far more than any animal (Matt. 6:25-33; Luke 12:4-7, 22-31; Matt. 12:12); because he taught from the perspective of one who knew and trusted God (John 6:41-51); and because he was a supreme master of the art of teaching.

One key to Jesus' success as a teacher was that he accepted persons for what they were and then challenged them to become what they had in them to become. To impetuous, unstable Peter he said: "Blessed are you, Simon Bar-Jona. . . . And I tell you, you are Peter, and on this rock I will build my church" (Matt. 16: 17-18). (See also his call of Nathaniel, John 1:43-50.) Note too his approach to the woman at the well of Samaria. Despite all her evil ways, he saw possibilities in her (John 4:1-42).

Another key to Jesus' greatness as a teacher was that he encouraged people to think; he did not tell them everything but left much of the initiative up to them; he asked searching, probing questions, which got them involved in the discussion. Thus did he encourage them to think and to act for themselves. When they sought to trap him with catch questions, he hurled back at them pointed questions, which got him off the hook and which taught most forcefully (Mark, ch. 12). His questions were sharply phrased.

—Whose likeness and inscription is this? (Mark 12:16).
—Why do you call me good? (Mark 10:18).
—Are you able to drink the cup that I drink, or to be baptized with the baptism with which I am baptized? (Mark 10:38).
—What man of you, if he has one sheep and it falls into a pit on the sabbath, will not lay hold of it and lift it out? (Matt. 12:11).
—And if Satan casts out Satan, he is divided against himself; how then will his kingdom stand? (Matt. 12:26).
—But who do you say that I am? (Luke 9:20).

Some of his greatest teachings were in answer to questions. In short, he took advantage of every teaching opportunity. A real question seriously asked is always a grand teaching opportunity, as many a wise parent knows. One said, "Who is my neighbor?" and he replied with the story of the good Samaritan. (Luke 10:29-37.) The disciples of John came to him, questioning, "Are you he who is to come, or shall we look for another?" and his reply was, "Go and tell John what you have seen and heard." (Luke 7:18-23.)

Jesus stressed activity. He put his disciples to work. Note the sending of the Twelve—and then of the seventy disciples—for specific purposes. (Luke 9:1-6, 10; 10:1-20.) Note the active words he used again and again: "go," "show," "tell," "feed," "do," "take," "wash," "heal," "preach," and "pray."

Jesus made use of what we would now call audio-visuals. Some of his miracles were clearly for teaching purposes. (The barren fig tree, Mark 11:12-14, 20-21; turning the water into wine, John 2:1-11.) His saying, "I am the light of the world" (John 8:12) took place at the Feast of Tabernacles, against the background of the great golden candlesticks, lighted on the first day of the feast. The Lord's Supper is the supreme audio-visual, the most powerful and the most vivid symbolism in all history. "This do in remembrance of me."

One seminary class for a given day was assigned the task of reading the Gospels (divided among the class) to see what teaching methods Jesus used. They came up with such ideas as these: he made brilliant use of questions, including countering one question by another; he aroused interest by means of shocking statements and paradoxes; he was a superb storyteller; he taught by demonstration—walking on the water to demonstrate faith in action; he *lived* his teaching; he taught by repetition—the same basic teachings recurring often ("For whoever would save his life will lose it" (Mark 8:35 and parallels); he utilized everything that came his way as a teaching opportunity—people's questions, tense situations, the great feasts, etc.; his teachings were directed to the immediate situation yet relevant beyond the situation; the needs of the people were primary. Not least, he taught through group dynamics. Jesus "appointed twelve, to be with him" (Mark 3:14). The master teacher with his little group was engaging in group dynamics long before men began to make a fetish of the idea. Any group studying the Gospels carefully would come up with some such list. The point is that Jesus really was a master of teaching, because he understood, respected, and loved people; because he led them to think; because he lived in vital relationship with his Father; and because he had something worth teaching. He taught with authority—with the authority of his person and of his teaching. Techniques were secondary, but still he used the best.

On Learning to Teach

In our limited space we cannot discuss teaching methods in detail. A group can easily spend ten, twenty, or thirty lesson periods discussing that topic, depending on how deeply they want to go into the subject. We hope that most of the users of this book will engage in serious study of teaching methods, both at the level of general principles and at the level of specific methods for use with a given age group. There are several basic ways in which prospective teachers can learn teaching methods.

1. The best single method of learning how to teach a given age group is to attend a "lab school." Such schools are usually available annually in large cities under the auspices of the council of churches, and at the state or regional level under the auspices of one's denomination. The essence of the lab method is that you learn to teach by observing an expert and then teaching under guidance. At present, lab school courses are mainly for teachers of kindergarten, primary, and junior children, though recently some schools have included courses for teachers of junior highs and senior highs. Many of the large church schools pay the expenses of teachers to attend lab schools. This is money well spent!

2. Another good method of learning is that of observation. You can, *with permission,* make several visits to a class of the age you expect to teach, to observe the teacher in action. You may even be able to visit a public-school class. The observer must observe unobtrusively.

3. Akin to observation is apprentice teaching in your own church. You are assigned to a competent teacher as substitute or as an assistant. You observe for a few Sundays, take over some minor duties, then finally you teach, and are given a friendly evaluation by the senior teacher. After a few months of this apprenticeship, you are ready to take on a similar class with confidence.

4. Take a course in a city or denominational leadership school. Or your orientation class, extended for a year, could spend a good number of periods on teaching methods, first in general, then by departments.

5. You can read books on teaching. There are a number of good books on teaching, some general, some for specific age groups. The following little books, which are both inexpensive and first-class, are highly recommended:

Kathrene McLandress Tobey, *When We Teach Kindergarten Children.* The Westminster Press, 1957.

Marjorie Haynes, *When We Teach Primary Children.* The Westminster Press, 1957.

Jane Bowerman Harris, *When We Teach Juniors.* The Westminster Press, 1957.

Sara Little, *Learning Together in the Christian Fellowship.* John
Knox Press, 1956. (For leaders of youth and adults, primarily
stressing newer group methods.)

In addition to these four fine books, an older series issued by
The Judson Press during the 1940's is still of real help. *Teaching
Intermediates,* by Lucile Desjardins (1940), is typical.

The main methods of teaching continue to be by telling, by
showing, and by doing. Some experts say that a child remembers
10 per cent of what he hears, 50 per cent of what he sees, and 90
per cent of what he does. These figures dramatically if exagger-
atedly remind us that some ways of teaching are more effective
than others. It is also true that different ways for different occasions are used. In fact, a good teacher may use more than one
teaching method in a given class period. The better the teacher
the more likely he is to use a variety of methods. (Exception: the
truly great lecturer.) We would urge beginning teachers to be
flexible in their teaching approach and to learn various techniques and methods. Most teachers can use some methods more
effectively than others, and they will tend to concentrate on those
methods. Within limits this is natural and good, but some variety
is helpful.

It needs to be added that we use different methods with different ages. Or more accurately, there is a general tendency to use a
different type of method with the older years, and even from age
group to age group the same method is used at different levels.
The story, for instance, is a universal method. For kindergarten
children the story is brief and simple, for junior highs it may be
far longer and less simple.

Solely for purposes of general information, let us make a hasty
survey of the teaching methods that are used at the various age
levels.

Nursery

The nursery age child learns primarily through the kind of relationships he experiences in church school, with adults and other
children. Formal teaching should never be tried with a nursery
class, but very small groups of two or three children can be taught
through conversation, simple stories, finger play, or songs. This
takes place informally as children come to the teacher, or as the

teacher joins the children at their play. It is as important for the teacher of nursery age children to be prepared and to have a plan and a purpose as for the teachers of older age groups. Teaching this age calls for maturity and seasoned wisdom.

Kindergarten

Play continues to be a main teaching tool. Toys, simple games, very informal dramatic play, and rhythm games are specific forms mentioned by Mrs. Tobey (*op. cit.*, pp. 30-47). Creative activities also are important at this age. (Not pasting for the sake of busy-work, but some form of truly creative activity in which the child draws or builds or paints something as he sees it, in connection with the study of the day.) Music is used, both in simple songs and in listening, and in rhythm for rest and relaxation. The conversational method is used, never the lecture. Conversation between adults and four- or five-year-old children is very informal. Surprising, humorous, and sometimes startling in insight are the questions and comments of children of this age. Stories are good when well told and not too long; always told, not read. The Bible is used at this age not so much to teach facts as to help create attitudes. Worship of a very informal sort also is used at this age.

Primary

Teachers of primaries use essentially the same methods that are used by teachers of kindergarten children but at levels deeper and more intensive. Here again the methods are geared to activity and involvement and are definitely informal in nature. Creative activities may be based upon the fact that the child is learning or has learned to read. There may be research committees to look up needed facts. Various manual activities related to the lesson are used. Dioramas, models of Biblical houses or temples, drawings to illustrate stories, murals, all are used with this age. Primaries may work out together a prayer or a poem. They may engage in dramatic activities informally and simply acting out some of the Biblical stories that are capable of being dramatized. Much use is made of music with primaries. Children of this age with skilled leadership have even written music. The story is, of course, still a major method. The discussion method or advanced conversation may be used with some groups on an informal basis.

Juniors

The nines to elevens are healthy and active and interested in amassing knowledge. They are mature enough for some solid work, memorizing Scripture, catechism, hymns, or prayers, learning how to use their Bibles rapidly and effectively, gaining a wide view of the Bible story. Juniors need and receive training in worship. They make abundant use of the methods of conversation and discussion. They like to reason if not to argue. Questions should be skillfully put to elicit thoughtful answers rather than an obvious yes or no. Juniors enjoy doing research and making reports. They can use maps and charts. Dramatization is their meat. They like to be creative in art and in writing. They will carry out projects. They need to be challenged and given plenty to do. They also need to have lots of fun, and their sense of humor is apt to be high. This is indeed a delightful age to teach.

Junior Highs

One form or another of discussion is usually the basic technique to use. Projects are fine with junior highs and senior highs. The junior high is enthusiastic but not stable, not yet ready for the long pull. His tasks must not be too long drawn out. Dramatizations have to be used with care, partly because this is the period of age differential between boy and girl. Girls at this age mature physically and socially about two years ahead of boys. If the junior high becomes interested and involved, he can learn a vast amount. An understanding teacher is more important here than skill in the use of methods.

Senior Highs and Above

The danger is that the lecture method will become the only method. The natural laziness of man leads both teacher and pupil to say, "I like the lecture method best." But for real teaching, some form of the discussion method ought to be used most of the time. Assignments and reports are always good if reminders are given. Senior highs may even be assigned to teach the lesson on occasion. Projects still have their place. With senior highs a more formal play takes priority over informal dramatization.

Adults

A good lecture is always acceptable to this group. As with senior highs, however, some form of group study is usually far more valuable. Some older adults are so satisfied with the lecture that it is almost impossible to use discussion. For purposes of information, introduction to a discussion, and inspiration, the lecture has a valuable place. The teacher of youth or adults, however, can be more successful with the newer group methods. Sara Little, in the table of contents of her book, lists the following methods of study: buzz groups, work groups, group discussion, panel, symposium, lecture, forums, listening teams, circular response, research and report, role-playing, plays, reading books, use of resource persons and materials, and use of the leadership team. The versatile and imaginative teacher can use most if not all these methods in the course of time.

Of Audio-Visuals

This ancient method of teaching has been blown up out of proportion to its value by some. The audio-visual that is used differs with the age. Flat pictures and class-made audio-visuals are more useful with the lower ages. Maps, charts, etc., click with juniors and above. Filmstrips and movies are primarily for juniors and above. The film and particularly the filmstrip when wisely used can be excellent teaching helps. The denominational teaching material usually recommends good films and filmstrips for use with particular lessons. Both record player and tape recorder, used imaginatively, can be of great value.

How to Teach This Lesson

If there is to be but one session on methods, then simply ask the class to read this chapter. During the class session bring out the main points by question and answer and by some form of discussion.

One class made this approach: first, a brief lecture by the leader on Jesus as a teacher; then a discussion of a specific illustration of his teaching technique (the woman at the well of Samaria, John 4:1-42); following this, four schoolteachers or veteran Sunday school teachers who were taking the class as refresher, made talks of ten minutes each on:

How we teach the preschool child.

How we teach the primary child (6–8).

How we teach the junior child (9–11).

How we teach youth (12–20).

Have members write out a complete plan for a given lesson, then get together in small groups to discuss good points and weaknesses of their lesson plans.

In a class that runs for six months or more, it would be good to devote one Sunday to the teaching methods for each main age group.

The Leadership Education Audio-Visual Kit (LEAV) (1950) includes several appropriate filmstrips, such as *The Teacher Prepares* and *The Teacher Teaches. The Youth Workers' Audio-Visual Kit* (1960) also offers valuable help. Both kits were produced co-operatively through the National Council of Churches.

IX

Curriculum Preview

Those who intend to take active leadership in the Christian education program of a particular church need to have an understanding of the curriculum that is used in that church. In a general sense, the curriculum is all that happens in a teaching situation—the teacher, the fellow pupils, the atmosphere, the room, the materials, even the total atmosphere of the local church. In the more restricted sense, the curriculum is the course of study, the lesson materials and other resource materials used to teach the Christian faith. It is in the more restricted sense that we use the term in this chapter. In an orientation course, the class should be taught specifically such facts as the nature of the curriculum being used, why it has been selected, who selected it, and how it can be supplemented. Customs differ widely in churches even of the same denomination. Some churches have a carefully selected curriculum that is followed by the entire church school; some have the chaotic situation in which each teacher selects his own curriculum. Order is better than chaos. New teachers and leaders need to know how and why order is preferable to unrestricted individualism.

Principles Underlying the Curriculum

As a general rule, a local church should use the curriculum worked out by its own denominational board of Christian education. The reasons for this are simple; as long as we have denominations we ought to be loyal to our own. The easy slipping from one denomination to another is likely to indicate shallowness rather than depth of Christian understanding. As firm believers in the ecumenical movement we recognize that the only good way to real unity is through each denomination bringing its treasures into the common storehouse, not through a watering down of the faith to the lowest common denominator. Both because of the need to offset mobility by continuity of program from church to church of the same denomination, and because the doctrine of the church revealed in a curriculum is of great importance, we strongly recommend that churches follow the curriculums of their respective denominations. There may be exceptions to this, but the basic principle is clear and sound. Where a church wishes to consider other possible curriculums, certain principles should be considered. The curriculum should:

1. Be unqualifiedly Christian in aim and in content.

2. Be rooted and grounded in the Bible, yet make adequate use of the history, beliefs, and current mission of the church.

3. Advocate the doctrine of the church integral to the denomination of which this congregation is a part.

4. Be based on educationally sound procedures, and be consistent with the nature of the gospel we teach. The teaching methods recommended should be both up to date and congenial to the teaching of the Bible to modern man. The curriculum should:

   a. Be properly graded so that it meets the needs of the pupils of each age group. The concept of developmental needs should be taken into consideration but evaluated Christianly.

   b. Follow the laws of the teaching-learning process and make these clear to the teachers.

5. Take into consideration both the home and the church as nurturing communities and make concrete and helpful suggestions of ways whereby home and church can work together in Christian nurture.

6. Contain material that is current, vital, and relevant to life in the atomic age, and face the issues of living with which the Christian must struggle in our time.

7. Be attractive, readable, usable literature that gives adequate help to the teachers.

8. Be constructed in accordance with the curriculum keys of balance, comprehensiveness, and sequence so that a student going through the departments of the church school will gain a steadily deepening understanding of God, and a richer comprehension of the meaning of Christian faith for growing persons in our era.

9. Be right in price. It is fairly certain that cheap literature is just that. You get what you pay for.

10. Be reasonably suited to the sociocultural level of the membership.

11. Help to make possible both knowledge about God in Jesus Christ and right relations with God and one's fellows.

Perhaps no curriculum meets all these criteria perfectly. But the curriculum that is used in a given church should meet as many of these criteria as possible.

No curriculum is any better than the persons who teach it. "The curriculum is 90 per cent teacher." That pardonable exaggeration contains so much truth that it explains why an orientation course is important. Good equipment helps. The best possible curriculum is advisable. But the teacher is the key to the use of equipment and materials.

Some pioneering spirits in Christian education are suggesting that no one denomination can possibly produce as many different curriculums as it ought to produce to meet the needs of the various types of churches in its constituency. Materials need to be prepared not only with age group structures in mind but also with social and cultural factors in mind. The isolated mountain community Sunday school probably cannot easily handle curriculum materials prepared by folk who are geared to the upper-middle-class suburbia type of church.

There is a common core in content and a common spirit in attitude in one's denominational curriculum. Although no denomination can produce materials fully suited for all types of churches, major denominations can produce materials that with skillful adaptation are usable in the vast majority of churches in the denomination. That is the present situation. Perhaps in the future some major denominations will produce co-operative curriculums for certain types of churches that do not fit into the average. But at present, the teacher has the responsibility of taking a curriculum for "the average church" and adapting it for his own church.

How Materials Are Selected

In many churches today there is a special committee that is responsible for the total educational program of the congregation, including the selection of curriculum materials. The official board (in the Presbyterian Church, for instance, the session) ultimately is responsible for the church school curriculum. Normally this responsibility is delegated to the committee on Christian education. After careful study of possible curriculums, the Christian education committee selects the material for its church, and upon formal approval by the official board this curriculum is adopted for use.

Many churches have a rule that once the curriculum has been decided upon, no teacher is permitted to discard upon his own decision the recommended curriculum. Only with the approval of the Christian education committee may a given teacher or a given department substitute another set of curriculum materials. The reason for this rule is that a curriculum is comprehensive and balanced and has a carefully worked out sequence. If in one department the curriculum is discarded and another curriculum used, then there is a gap in materials and in experience which may be difficult to overcome. The materials are planned to complement and supplement and develop toward a common goal with carefully planned stages.

Once the decision is made as to which curriculum is to be used it does not need to be reviewed annually, though perhaps every six or twelve years such a review is indicated.

Although it is not wise for a given teacher to teach his or her own materials without regard to the curriculum adopted for the church school, it is tremendously important for every teacher to use supplementary materials as needed. No good teacher is bound by a printed curriculum, for he is ever on the alert for fresh materials that will help him teach the Christian religion most effectively to his class.

We should distinguish carefully between the absurd atomistic individualism of letting each teacher choose his own curriculum materials and the educationally sound policy of encouraging each teacher to use initiative, ingenuity, and imagination in adapting or modifying materials to meet the needs of his students. It is mere legalism to insist that a teacher must teach X lesson on December 13 and Y lesson on December 20, when he may realize that X lesson is so meaningful for his class that he must continue it on December 20. The wise teacher makes flexible use of his materials. For the older years undated materials become increasingly attractive. The tendency is to electives for adults, but these electives are within a comprehensive plan, not merely indiscriminate electives.

How to Teach This Lesson

If your church has adopted the denominational materials, it may well be that your denominational board has prepared materials which give an over-all preview of the curriculum. The United Presbyterian Church in the U.S.A., for instance, has a film-strip, *The Versatile Vehicle,* which does an admirable job of giving a broad interpretation of the nature of the curriculum, its purposes, its three main themes, its divisions, its various study books, and parent-teacher magazines and supplementary materials. Most denominations have printed materials that give a broad interpretation of the curriculum. Certainly no person should start to teach until he has some idea of the purpose of the curriculum, its scope, its major themes, its divisions, etc. This session should give such an interpretation, through audio-visuals if possible, or through printed materials, and through discussion or question and answer. A teacher needs to know that careful thought has been given to what comes after what, and to have in perspective the total curriculum as well as the material his own class will use on a given Sunday.

Write your denominational headquarters (national or regional) for suggestions concerning an interpretation of the curriculum to a leadership class.

X

Introduction to Christian Doctrine

The brevity of this chapter has no relationship to its importance. In the generation prior to 1945, it was the fashion even among ministers to make sneering remarks about theology. There was little theological or doctrinal preaching and as a result the foundations of American church life became shaky. The second great World War with its revelation of the depths to which men could sink, along with the dropping of the atom bomb, chastened the overly optimistic, unduly shallow thinking of pulpit and pew alike. Both in Christian education and in preaching there has been a revitalization of theology. It *does* make a difference what a man believes. The excessive individualism of Protestantism run wild, in which every man's belief is considered to be as good as every other man's belief, and little if any thought is given to the beliefs of the Christian church as such, has been corrected. We know now that Christians inescapably are part of the church and that the traditions and doctrines of the church, while not infallible, do have a great deal to say to the modern Christian as he wrestles with his own beliefs. Instead of saying one man's ideas are as good as another's, we now recognize that the burden of proof is on the man whose ideas depart greatly from the ideas of the church. This is a more conservative note than formerly was heard, but it's a needed corrective.

It may be true that "this is not an age of theology," but it is equally true that "man in his thoughtful moments becomes something of a theologian." Laymen in our churches today will do as much theological thinking as they are guided to do. There is, we have found, a deep hunger on the part of laymen for sound answers to theological questions. Long have college students been theologically concerned, but now the rank-and-file layman asks intelligent questions and wants honest and intelligent answers. After all, life's fundamental questions are theological.

This hunger for theological understanding is sometimes inarticulate and unrecognized, but wherever a good minister gives his people meat as well as milk, they want more and more and are eager to wrestle with fundamental issues. Twelve years in university church pastorates convinced us of this, but we have seen it emphasized anew in an average congregation in recent years. Given a chance, people want to dig into serious questions. Sometimes for some people this is just another form of escape from facing the social issues of the day. But this hunger goes deeper than escapism; it is a genuine need of the questioning human spirit.

There are two aspects to the matter of theology: on the one hand, the common core of Christian theology that is held by all the main-line denominations and by most of the sects; and on the other hand, the unique or special denominational emphases. Laymen want answers in both spheres, particularly laymen who expect to take their places as leaders in the life of the church. Future church school officers and teachers rightly want to have some grasp of the doctrinal teachings of the Christian church and also of their own denomination. And some who are not aware of this need actually are likely to be particularly in need of help.

One year in the experimental class that led to the writing of this book, we spent an hour in class discussing basic Christian beliefs, then two extra two-hour sessions were held at night. Each year when opportunity is given for discussion of theological questions, extra sessions at night are desired.

We strongly believe that all church leaders should become familiar with the basic Christian beliefs, and also with the particular doctrinal tenets that distinguish their own denomination. The people who are more perceptive want this, for they know their need. And the church needs this, for it can be most disruptive to have church school teachers whose theology is no more than a high-grade humanism. It is extremely doubtful that a Unitarian should assume a place of active leadership in a confessional church that holds to a Trinitarian understanding of God. The sort of teacher whose basic purpose is to teach good character, good conduct, good morals, ought to be eliminated from our church schools. For, while the Christian ethic cuts deep, to remain at the level of character development is to do no more than the public school or any secular character-building agency, and to surrender the fundamental God-centered or Christocentric nature of the gospel. Extreme fundamentalist teachers are as dangerous to the peace and harmony of a confessional church as are extreme liberal teachers. It is not the purpose of these periods on doctrine to become heresy-hunting times, but these periods should lead to such clarification of the basic Christian beliefs and of the denomination's own cherished convictions, that a person taking the course will have a clear idea as to whether or not he really has a right to be teaching in this particular church.

The point is not to say, "If you don't believe this, you can't teach," but rather to say: "This is what the church believes. Before you start teaching, we suggest that you come to an understanding of what it is you are to teach and to know the danger zones. If you have trouble with a major doctrine, then sit down with your pastor for a conference on this matter. Perhaps he can clear things up for you." Even if a few conscientious persons are lost to the teaching force because they consider themselves far too liberal, or far too fundamentalist, for this congregation, in the end there will be a better, more solidly based teaching force.

It is not to be expected that the new church school teacher will have a complete knowledge of theology when he starts. But he ought not to start until he knows the wheat from the chaff in theological questions. Just as he should grow in his understanding of the Bible during his teaching years, so should he *grow* in his understanding of Christian theology.

The church school teacher is not expected to be a technical theologian, but he is expected to be a sincere believer in the essentials of the Christian faith. His personal faith may be very simple, or it may be very profound, but it must be genuine. This does not mean that he will have no doubts. Practically all Christians who are honest with themselves will confess to having times when God seems far removed, or unreal, or times when prayer seems meaningless and God's providence seems questionable. For faith that is alive always is in tension with the very real possibilities of doubt. In our kind of world most men have at least flashes of doubt. As Tennyson well knew, there is faith in honest doubt.

Some of this theologizing should be about the living theology of the church and not about creedal documents per se. What is the theology of stewardship, of sex, of vocation, of evangelism, of race relations, of politics? That there is no clear-cut party line for all Christians on all of these items will surprise some laymen. They need to learn to think in the context of the freedom of the church to be the church in its own day and generation and of the individual Christian's freedom to think Christianly within the context of the life of the people of God.

How to Teach This Lesson

In the Appendix we give a "theology quiz" that we have found to be extremely useful as a starter for theological discussion. With us it always took at least four hours, for we allowed discussion wherever desired, with different points of view frankly expressed. The leader where advisable gave his interpretation of the common mind of the church after the question had been discussed. This quiz is a good starting point. It has a certain ambiguity on occasion that makes for discussion. Some will prefer to work out their own questions.

Another possibility for this class period is to break the class into small groups and assign to each group the asking and the answering of what to them are the basic theological questions in a given area, say, God, Jesus Christ, salvation, eternal life, etc.

In a creedal church, the minister may be requested to lead a forum on his denomination's interpretation of some of the great Christian doctrines. Ideally, in such a church, there would be a three-month course on the theme, instead of just one period. All members should be urged to read their denomination's creed or confession of faith prior to a forum or discussion period on it.

Yet another possibility would be to assign to particularly well-qualified persons in the group the task of reporting briefly on a particular doctrine. A fit topic would be, "Who is Jesus Christ as the church sees him today?" A noncreedal church might wish to approach a doctrinal discussion through the teachings of the most-used hymns on a given theological doctrine. The ways of approach to theological discussion are limited solely by the imagination of the teacher and the class. The need for a theology of sex could be seen by a study of the local paper for a week, or a study of the movies shown in your town during a month. And so with other living theological questions.

The writers are convinced that either the pastor or the DCE

should teach these lessons on Christian beliefs, unless there is a well-qualified layman available. And by "well-qualified layman" we mean not simply one who is distinguished in his own vocation, but one who is also and fundamentally distinguished for his understanding of Christian doctrine and his devotion to the church and its Lord. Such laymen do exist, and more should be trained by able pastors.

At least two periods should be devoted to this topic, probably divided into a discussion of general Christian beliefs and a discussion of one's denominational beliefs.

XI

Policies and Practices for Organizing and Administering the Christian Education Program

The purpose of this session is to show the members of the class the organizational structure of the Christian education program in their particular church and to acquaint them with the basic principles of organization and administration that are followed.

We live in the era of the organization man, and though we poke fun at the idea, all of us are caught by it. We are creatures of our culture, and our culture demands much emphasis on organization, much emphasis on conformity, and much skill in administrative techniques through stress on interpersonal relations and "togetherness." We have too much organization and too many of us spend too much time keeping the wheels going around instead of doing the more important things. Yet no institution can exist for long without organization, not even a human body. The body that is the church likewise has to be organized, with various members carrying out their respective functions for the good of all. To be disorganized is to be malfunctioning. To be organized is to function with health or wholeness. To be overorganized is to be caught and frustrated as was the famous centipede that got to thinking which leg came after which and became so confused he fell into the ditch. But organization is essential if we are to do the work of Christians in our time in our country.

The church school, like the church, has to have an organization. And this organizational complex has to be ad*ministere*d. Note the italics. Administration is a form of ministering, and ministering is service. One of the main functions of the modern pastor is to be an administrator—administering the total church program including Christian education—ministering to the people through this process. It is customary for cynics to talk scathingly of pastors spending too much time in administration and too little time in study, and of some pastors the criticism is valid. But every pastor has to be an administrator.

No pastor has to do the job alone. He has a church official board or a church council, whether it be called the session, the diaconate, the board of stewards, or the vestry. These men (and women) share with him the tasks of administration. Further, he and they should train other laymen to assume administrative functions and should delegate responsibility to such trained laymen. That is why you are in this leadership class!

The chart opposite shows the flow of authority and of responsibility. Some denominations would begin with the congregation; others would start with the denomination itself. All, ultimately, begin with the church universal, and its head, Jesus Christ. Well-organized churches can carry out these functions without too many conflicts or too many pulls upon a given individual.

Some Principles of Organization and Administration

1. Organization and administration exist not to keep the wheels running but to enable the church to carry out its life and mission. Christ is the head, and each organ has its place in the structure and functioning of the whole body.

2. Organization helps achieve the unity of the body. Each part of the body must recognize that it is a part of the whole and cannot go its own way. Violation of this simple rule has caused many people to have bad cases of "Sunday schoolitis," or "auxiliaryitis," or "bowlingteamitis" or "choiritis."

3. Where the body is well organized, all its parts are carrying out their properly assigned functions. The purpose of church organization is to help as many members as possible to make their contributions to the ongoing life of the church. This is not to say that every Christian ought to teach Sunday school; it is most emphatically not to say that every Christian ought to belong to every possible organization in the church and accept whatever leadership challenges are offered. Some people ought not to try to teach, others ought not to try to sing in the choir, and few ought to try to do both. Some people take so many positions in the church that

A Typical Organizational Chart

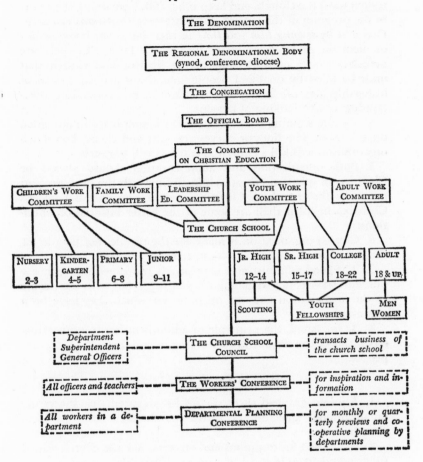

they get spiritual indigestion, give their children a negative attitude toward the church, and keep other folk from doing their part in the program of the church. Further, *some Christians can serve God best by serving him full time in their vocation;* home or law or medicine or labor union or business or farm. But there are necessary places of leadership in the institutional church that must be filled by qualified people, and the wider the spread of leadership here the better. There should be no overloading, overlapping, or overlooking of persons.

4. Despite seeming complexity, there is simplicity in any good organization. The lines or curves are clear and clean. Too much organization will kill a church as easily as will too little.

5. Both organization and administration should always be Christian in spirit and in principle, in line with the purposes and nature of the church. A Christian organization dare not be less Christian in spirit than are some of the better business organizations.

6. Church organization is made for the people, not people for the institutional church and its structures.

7. The good administrator is primarily concerned not with size but with service, not with organization per se but with the people in the organization and the purposes for which they have been organized.

8. As indicated, the principle of administration is ministering, servanthood, the servant Lord working in and through his servant people.

How to Teach This Lesson

1. A mimeographed sheet should be prepared that shows the organizational structure of Christian education in your local church.

2. Some time for questions and answers. Ask the church school superintendent to lead this discussion, if feasible.

3. The superintendent, or the chairman of the Christian education committee, might well set forth some of the ground rules that every worker ought to understand. One church, for instance, has such ground rules as:

—only the secretary will order curriculum materials;
—only department superintendents can charge materials needed in class or project;

—only the Christian education committee can invite a person to teach a class; no teacher may quit and ask another person to take his place;

—the church guarantees to furnish the best materials and equipment; the teacher promises to give adequately of time and energy and thought, to do his task well;

—most business matters are handled by the Sunday school council; teachers meetings (workers conferences) are for information and inspiration;

—only the Christian education committee can choose the curriculum, subject to the session.

The reasons for the ground rules of a particular congregation should be stated clearly and discussed as needed. Ground rules may be changed from time to time, but by official action after due discussion, not by irresponsible unilateral action.

4. "What the church expects of its workers" could be discussed, either by a panel or by a talk from a member of the Christian education committee.

5. The roles and functions of the following persons should be made clear to the group: the pastor, the director of Christian education, and the church school superintendent.

6. The way in which the Christian education program is financed should be explained.

XII

The Dedicated Christian Educator

In the last analysis, the Christian education program of a particular church depends more on the quality of its teachers than on anything else. Supremely important in this regard is the matter of dedication. If a teacher is dedicated to his task, and happy in the doing of it, he will have real influence and do a great deal of good. If he lacks that commitment, no matter how attractive his personality or how well equipped his mind, he will not be apt to have a profound effect upon the lives of his pupils. The dedication of our teachers is therefore of utmost importance.

Protestants have taken seriously the Biblical teaching that all believers have a share in the corporate priesthood of the church. There is no need of priests, since Jesus Christ, the great high priest, has entered into the sanctuary and offered up the perfect sacrifice, once and for all. Yet the church as his body continues to exercise a priestly ministry and we as individual members thereof share that priesthood. We do not have to go to God through the mediation of a cultic, sacrificing priest, but we can directly approach the throne of grace. The universal priesthood of all believers also means that we offer intercession for one another. Christians have a priestly ministry one to the other.

Let it be said emphatically that although the church school arose as a layman's movement, it is obvious today that the Christian education of the church demands the skilled professional leadership of a minister or a DCE. The ministry is a gift of God to the church (Eph. 4:11) and presumably a permanent gift. "Some to be pastors and teachers" defines the role of the minister concisely. He is the main teacher of the church, and when he unfolds the word of God honestly and truly, he is to be listened to and the word he unfolds is to be obeyed. *His task is terrific.* We need the best possible ministers, who will give the finest possible leadership, but the minister cannot do it all. Nor should he attempt to do so. It is not unheard of for a Protestant minister to be as dictatorial as some Roman Catholic priests are reputed to be. The wise pastor is never a dictator, nor does he wish to be. He is servant of God first and then of God's people. If perchance a minister is unwise and dictatorial, then the laity usually let him run things, assuming little responsibility and often bearing a deep resentment.

The principle of the priesthood of believers, or in modern terminology "the ministry of the laity," ought never to be interpreted to mean that the laity can now take over everything and get rid of ordained ministers. Neither ought it to be interpreted that laity and clergy are natural enemies. In some quarters today a misguided effort is being made to drive a wedge between the laity and the ordained ministers. The end of this can be only chaos and ultimate degeneration of the church. The glory of the church is when laity and clergy are genuinely one in Christ, colaborers with him. Let it never be forgotten that the word "laity" comes from *laos,* people, the people of God, and therefore the minister too is part of the *laos* of God and serves God where he has been set.

The true meaning of the priesthood of believers is that all Christians share in the priestly ministry of Christ, mutually interceding for one another and for the church. The ministry of the laity is to be carried out not simply on Sunday but primarily on the other six days of the week. The Christian calling is to discipleship. The ministry of the laity is to serve God in office and in factory, in field and in home, in school and in business—there bearing witness to God's gracious love in Jesus Christ by life and by deed. The lay Christian's ministry is to serve God where he has been placed.

In addition to this general service of the laity, some are called to serve him in specific places in his church.

Now that you have taken this orientation course, in all probability you will be asked to take on a specific assignment for Christian leadership. Perhaps already you have accepted the assignment. Certain things follow. The dedicated Christian teacher normally will:

1. Be faithful and regular. An irregular teacher may do harm

by giving the class the idea that it comes second to many other interests in the life of the teacher. If you accept a class, do so with the expectation of being regular in attendance. The teacher who opened his class with the words, "I'd lots rather be hunting squirrels," lost those high school youth then and there!

2. Be prompt and on time each Sunday. "The lesson begins when the first child arrives," is an old saying of children's workers. Particularly in the children's division, teachers should arrive about fifteen minutes before the church school is supposed to open. All teachers should be present, calm and collected, and ready to begin promptly. This encourages pupils to be prompt too.

3. Be prepared for each lesson. Some people think they can get away with little preparation, but you can fool folk, particularly children, only for a little while. The amount of preparation varies greatly with the present knowledge of the teacher, the age of the class, and the curriculum. But every lesson should be adequately prepared. One elder we know used to prepare his lesson on the bus en route to work, twenty minutes each way, five days a week. You can find the time for preparation, or you are too busy. The beginning teacher should have a lesson outline carefully prepared, though the good teacher always uses an outline flexibly.

Such preparation involves faithful study of the Bible and of supplementary materials. It involves also a growing understanding of the persons you teach, through personal knowledge of their homes, their background, etc.

4. Live with your Bible so that its language and, most of all, its meaning and message become a living part of your being.

5. Be active in the total life of the Christian community. Do not try to do everything in the church, but what you do, do well. By all means, the church school teacher needs to be most faithful in attendance upon common worship. This he should do primarily because he needs to worship God in company with his fellows, and secondarily that he may set an example.

6. Become a team player. Learn to work with others. Bring your personal idiosyncrasies, your pet peeves, your self-centeredness under control of the Christian spirit of love and unity. Pray to be delivered from combative self-assertiveness, easily hurt feelings, and self-righteousness. Be a healthy cell in the body of Christ!

7. Be a growing teacher. One grows through wider acquaint-

ance with life and its issues in our age, through deepening knowledge of the Scriptures and of the persons we teach, and through a steady and faithful dependence upon God in prayer.

8. Be dependent upon the power and leading of the Holy Spirit.

Even the most dedicated Christian teacher will have times of discouragement. Teaching is rewarding, but often the rewards do not come until years later, when a lad now become a man tells you how a certain thing you said to him changed his life. We once heard the late Dr. James Black preach an Easter sermon on I Cor. 15:58. He told this story: One day while on the New York subway he fell into conversation with a fellow-straphanger. When the man learned that Dr. Black was a minister, he said: "I teach a Sunday school class myself. I have twelve junior boys. And I think I am going to quit. They are so wiggly and so inattentive that I just don't feel like I am succeeding with them. I'm awfully discouraged." Dr. Black looked at the young man a moment and replied: "Don't forget that our Lord took twelve and taught them. He too was discouraged at times, but he didn't quit."

"I appeal to you therefore, brethren, by the mercies of God, to present your bodies [selves] as a living sacrifice, holy and acceptable to God, which is your spiritual worship." (Rom. 12:1.)

How to Teach This Lesson

This last session could well be turned into a review of the most significant points the class has gained from the course. Proceed by way of informal discussion or by way of buzz groups.

Either at the beginning or at the end of the class, use the filmstrip from the LEAV Kit entitled *The Growing Teacher*.

APPENDIX

Theology Quiz for Teachers

The statements that follow express various points of view on various aspects of religious beliefs. Some represent issues on which there may be honest difference of opinion. You are asked to give your judgment on each of the statements. The record of your judgment may help you gain a clearer picture of your present religious thinking.

With respect to each statement you may AGREE, DISAGREE, be UNCERTAIN, or express NO OPINION at all. "Uncertain" means that you understand the statement but do not know whether you agree with it or not, or that you agree with only part of the statement. "No opinion" is distinguished from uncertainty; it indicates that the statement is not meaningful to you, or that it is phrased in a way that makes it seem ambiguous, or that you cannot express an opinion on it without implying the acceptance of some assumption which you do not care to grant, or that you cannot express judgment upon it.

Whichever one of these four reactions you make to a statement, you may wish to indicate a desire for further information about some statements or for having them discussed in a forthcoming teachers meeting.

Read each statement carefully. Mark your reaction at the right: (1) Agree, (2) Disagree, (3) Uncertain, (4) No opinion.

DO YOU BELIEVE THAT

I. CONCERNING GOD
    1. God is our Father, long-suffering, merciful, just, and infinitely kind ...._____

2. God is a person ...._____

3. God is best understood as the spiritual principle behind the universe ...._____

4. We may know what God is like from nature
   and human life in general ...._____

5. We depend for our knowledge of God on
   his revelation in Jesus Christ ...._____

6. God is triune: Father, Son, and Holy
   Spirit ...._____

7. The guidance of the Holy Spirit is necessary for Christian life today ...._____

8. There is a spark of God in every man to
   which his Spirit can speak directly ...._____

9. Everybody has some kind of theology, which
   is revealed in everything he says about
   religion ...._____

10. A concern with creeds is detrimental to a
    living experience of God ...._____

11. The same theological principles should
    govern what is taught young children and
    mature persons ...._____

II. CONCERNING JESUS CHRIST

1. God sent his Son Jesus Christ to be the
   Savior of the world ...._____

2. Man is lost and in need of a savior ...._____

3. Jesus saves men by teaching them the way
   of the good life ...._____

4. Jesus saves men by taking away their sins on
   the cross and opening up eternal life by his
   resurrection ...._____

5. Jesus can be best understood as the greatest
   moral teacher ...._____

6. Jesus is merely the finest example of man's
   possible development ...._____

7. Jesus is God appearing in human flesh ...._____

8. Jesus was also perfectly human, suffering all
   the weaknesses of flesh and blood, yet with-
   out sin ...._____

9. What we believe about Jesus is not important for the purpose of becoming his dis-
   ciples ...._____

10. In teaching children about their Savior, the convictions and examples of adults nearest to them are of the greatest importance ...._____

III. CONCERNING THE BIBLE

1. It is a record of man's search for God ...._____

2. It brings us God's self-revelation in Jesus Christ ...._____

3. The purpose of God's revelation in Christ is to impart certain facts, ideas, and moral truths ...._____

4. The Old Testament is not as valuable as the New Testament ...._____

5. The Old Testament testifies to the very same grace, mercy, promise, judgment, and power that became incarnate in Jesus of Nazareth ...._____

6. Bible-teaching should be mainly factual, without application to social and political problems today ...._____

7. All questions of life can be answered by looking up specific verses of Scripture ...._____

8. Every part of the Bible is directly inspired by God, and man had nothing to do with it _____

9. Every writer was inspired by God, but he spoke out of his experience ...._____

10. One's interpretation of any part of the Bible should be made in the light of the findings of Biblical and literary criticism ...._____

11. It is the Word of God, with supernatural revelation for spiritual guidance of mankind ...._____

12. It contains the one way of salvation and is authoritative for all Christians ...._____

IV. CONCERNING THE CHURCH

1. The church is primarily a social institution organized by men of good will on their own initiative ...._____

2. The Christian church is a divine-human society that God has ordained for the redemption of mankind ...._____

3. The church is the greatest single agency for good in the world ...._____

4. The purpose of missions is to develop world brotherhood ...._____

5. The church must engage in evangelistic work, because of God's concern for people_____

6. The purpose of preaching and teaching in the church is to bring persons face to face with God in Christ ...._____

7. The sacraments of Baptism and the Lord's Supper are essential in the life of the church ...._____

8. The work of the church could be just as effectively done by the schools and social agencies ...._____

9. The church should become more actively interested in social and economic questions_____

10. There are basic differences within the church that form an impossible barrier to a united Christian front ...._____

11. The church needs a new spirit of repentance and faith to fulfill God's will in today's world ...._____

A Select Bibliography

The following list of books is given top priority, each for a different reason. Some excellent books have been omitted for brevity's sake. Each book here mentioned should be in the church library. The pastor may have several of these. Books on theology, Biblical theology, and psychology have been omitted. The leadership education department of each denominational board of Christian education can recommend excellent pamphlets on various phases of the subject. A book marked with an asterisk is a "must."

BOWMAN, CLARICE M., *Ways Youth Learn*. Harper & Brothers, 1952.

CULLY, IRIS V., *Children in the Church*. The Westminster Press, 1960.

*——— *The Dynamics of Christian Education*. The Westminster Press, 1958.

FAIRLY, JOHN L., and ARLEENE G., *Using the Bible to Answer Questions Children Ask*. John Knox Press, 1958.

FEUCHT, OSCAR E., ed., *Helping Families Through the Church*. Concordia Publishing House, 1957.

FOREMAN, KENNETH J., *et al., Introduction to the Bible*. The Layman's Bible Commentary, Vol. 1. John Knox Press, 1959.

FOSTER, VIRGIL E., *How a Small Church Can Have Good Christian Education*. Harper & Brothers, 1956.

*GABLE, LEE J., *Christian Nurture Through the Church*. National Council of the Churches of Christ in the U.S.A., 1955.

——— ed., *Encyclopedia for Church Group Leaders*. Association Press, 1959.

GETTYS, JOSEPH M., *How to Teach the Bible*. John Knox Press, 1949.

GRIMES, HOWARD, *The Church Redemptive*. Abingdon Press, 1958.

*HOWE, REUEL L., *Man's Need and God's Action*. The Seabury Press, Inc., 1953.

KRAEMER, HENDRIK, *The Communication of the Christian Faith*. The Westminster Press, 1956.

*LITTLE, SARA, *Learning Together in the Christian Fellowship*. John Knox Press, 1956.

LOVE, JULIAN PRICE, *How to Read the Bible*. The Macmillan Company, rev. ed., 1959.

MILLER, RANDOLPH C., *Education for Christian Living*. Prentice-Hall, Inc., 1956.

REEVES, MARJORIE, *Growing Up in a Modern Society*. University of London Press, London, 4th ed., 1956.

*SHERRILL, LEWIS J., *The Gift of Power*. The Macmillan Company, 1955.

———— *The Rise of Christian Education*. The Macmillan Company, 1944.

*———— *The Struggle of the Soul*. The Macmillan Company, 1951.

SMART, JAMES D., *The Teaching Ministry of the Church*. The Westminster Press, 1954.

*TAYLOR, MARVIN J., ed., *Religious Education*. Abingdon Press, 1960.

VIETH, PAUL H., *The Church School*. Christian Education Press, 1957.

WYCKOFF, D. CAMPBELL, *The Gospel and Christian Education*. The Westminster Press, 1959.

———— *The Task of Christian Education*. The Westminster Press, 1955.

YEAXLEE, BASIL A., *Religion and the Growing Mind*. The Seabury Press, Inc., 1952.

Index

Administration of Christian education, 123 ff.

Adolescence, 66, 87–89, 110

Adults: are teachers, 44; how teach, 111; need to be taught, 13, 51, 56–57, 67–68

Audio-visuals, 111

Bible: an adult book, 67–69; central, 59; contains record of revelation, 60; a divine-human book, 60–61; a genuine unity, 63; and the Holy Spirit, 61, 67; not an end in itself, 65–66; not on one level, 62; place of N.T., 64; place of O.T., 63–64; primary curriculum tool, 59, 67 f.; to be read in faith, 61–62; a revelation from God to man, 59; taught to children, 69; teachers and, 65, 67; that we may encounter God, 69; youth needs to know, 66

Book of Common Worship, 55

Buber, Martin, 18

Calvin, John, 37, 38–39, 54, 67, 76

Catechism, 14, 15

Change, 91, 92, 99–102

Childhood, 52–53, 69–70, 108, 109–110

Children and the church, 70

Christian doctrine, 118–121

Christian education: defined, 20; history, 14–15, 50; importance, 11 ff.; lifelong, 36, 46; nature, 16–19, 36–37; scope, 13–14

Church, the fellowship of learning: a community, 30; community of the Holy Spirit, 38 ff.; as covenant community, 39, 53, 55; its divinity, 39–40; its humanity, 40; its notes, 40–43; its unity, 38, 42–43; as a school, 45–46; teaches by its whole life, 43–45

Communication: current hindrances to, 21–25; its nature, 25; meaning of words, 25–29; as obedience, 33; occurs in community, 30, 36; place of Holy Spirit, 34; a two-way street, 32; what happens during, 29 ff.

Community: characteristics, 37 f.; defined, 37. *See also* Church: as covenant community

Concern, 41–42

Conditioned response, 95–97

Conformity, 22–23

Confrontation, 16–19, 33. *See also* Encounter